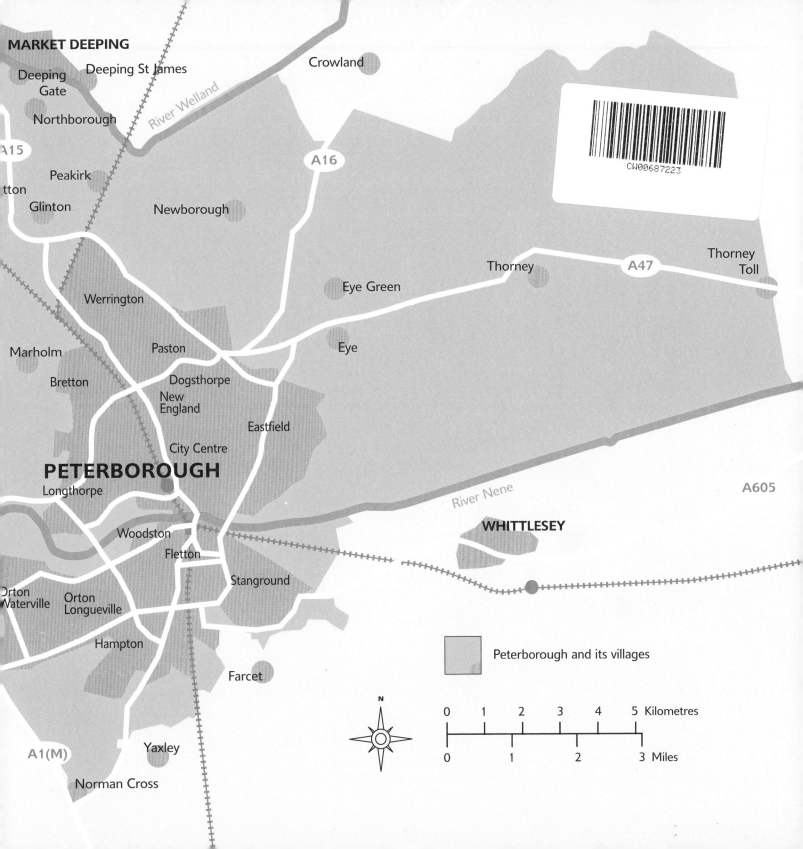

Peterborough
and its villages
in detail

First published in Great Britain by Peterborough Civic Society
Registered UK Charity Number 279306
© Peterborough Civic Society 2012
www.peterborough.net/civicsociety
ISBN 978-1-907750-35-9
Designed and produced by Jigsaw Design & Publishing Ltd, Norwich.
Design by Kaarin Wall
Printed in Great Britain. 11045-1/12

Peterborough

and its villages

in detail

Foreword by Griff Rhys Jones

Acknowledgements

Peterborough Civic Society gratefully acknowledges
grant assistance and encouragement from the following:

Revd Richard Paten

The Earl Fitzwilliam Charitable Trust

Peterborough Decorative and Fine Arts Society

Cross Keys Homes

Toby Wood

The Society also records its thanks to:

Peterborough Photographic Society for its vigorous support throughout.

Richard Deane of Salisbury Civic Society for generously sharing information on
the production of their book *Salisbury in Detail*, the inspiration for this project.

Dave Holman – piloting for aerial photography.

Peterborough Visitor Information Centre and www.visitpeterborough.com

Vivacity Peterborough for general support.

Malcolm Crampton and Kaarin Wall of Jigsaw Design and Publishing Ltd
for advice and guidance, design and printing.

The Peterborough in Detail Working Group

David Jost, Henry Mansell Duckett, Tony Knighton, Peter Lee, Toby Wood
Peterborough Civic Society

David Good, Richard Houghton, Liz Kemp
Peterborough Photography Society

Alice Kershaw
Peterborough Heritage Regeneration Officer

Sarah Wilson
Vivacity Peterborough – Museums and Heritage

Contents

Subscribers   6

The Photographers and Author   7

Foreword   9

Introduction   11

Gateways and Doors   12

Boot-scrapers   28

Steeples, Towers, Turrets and Cupolas   32

Gables and Pediments   40

Windows   52

Arcading   72

Door and Window Heads   78

Window Tracery   88

Chimneys and Roof Details   100

Rainwater Heads, Gutters and Downpipes   122

Brick, Stone and Terracotta   126

Clockfaces and Sundials   140

Carvings   146

Ironwork and Ironmongery   160

Street Furniture   172

Coats of Arms and Plaques   180

Signs and Lettering   188

A Miscellany   196

Afterword   216

The Subscribers

We would like to thank the following subscribers for their support by means of advance purchase ahead of publication.

Lise Alexander-Smith
Susan Anstruther
Dick Arnold
Richard Astle
Athene Communications
Robert Atkin
Axiom Housing Association
Derek & Diane Ball
Bill Bateman
David Bath
Peter Beasley
Paul Biggins
Rex & Anne Birchenough
Roy W Bird MBE & Mrs Norma Bird
Justin & Scilla Blake-James
Peter Boizot MBE
David Bond
Mrs Karina Bonnett
Steve Boorman & Rosy Calvert
Sarah Botfield
Martin Bradshaw
Anne & Mick Bream
Barbara & Derek Brett
Mr Anthony Buckingham
Mrs Ruth Buckingham
Richard & Elizabeth Bulkeley
June & Vernon Bull
Margot & Norman Burden
Mrs Judith F Bunten
Barry Butler
Robert, Brenda, Michael
    & Janet Chamberlain
Gordon Chambers
Meg Chandler
Civic Society of St Ives
JA & KF Clarke
James Cook
Christopher Cooper
Mr RP Cousins
Sarah Cresswell
Cross Keys Homes
Mrs Jean Crouchman
Dr Nicola Curtis & Dr Andrew Curtis

Margaret D'Arcy
Mr & Mrs JR D'Arcy
Dr & Mrs Tom Davies
Kerry & Adrian Davies
Roger & Vivienne Davis
Michael E Delegate
Dr Beryl Dennis
Richard Donoyou
Tony & Winnie Dwight
Janet & David Dykes
Janine Dykes
Samantha East
Engineering Services Partnership Ltd
Mr & Mrs AJT Evans
June Yvonne Farrer-Western
Daphne M Faux
William Faux
Mr John Field
Marian Freeman & Robin Freeman
Clive & Janet Frusher
Alison Fure
Clive & Hilary Gallup
Keith Garrett
Edie Garvie
Mr Brian Gibson
Gladstone Primary School
Dr Ross & Helen Gordon
Alan Gowler
D & S Halfhide
Duncan & Patricia Hallam
O & H Hampton Ltd
Steve & Ann Hanson
Peter Harvey
Peter Hawes
Mr & Mrs CW Haythornthwaite
Kath & David Henderson
Hereward Homes Ltd
Jennifer Hibbard
Cllr Peter Hiller
Mr & Mrs R Hillier
Mrs B Hirst
Jim & Jane Hogg
Cllr John Holdich OBE

Mike Holland
Mel Holley
Marcus Horrell
Karin Horsley
Anne Horspole
Mr David Hufford
Rex & Liz Humphrey
Peter & Avril Hurst
RG & BG Hutton
John Clare Cottage
Stephen Johnston
Richard M Jones
Judy Jones & Karen Osborne
Janice A Jones
Emily Jost
Marion Julyan
Roger Kernow
Brian & Hilary Keegan
Jacqueline & Peter Knaggs
Tony & Mavis Knighton
Mick & Alison Langford
John & Louise Lawrence
Cllr Matthew Lee
Peter & Janet Lee
Martin Lightfoot
Jean & Ted Little
Mr & Mrs BW Long
Stephanie & Don Low
Douglas & Pat Maltman
Mrs Pat Manders
Colin & Marion Marshall
David & Valerie McDermott
Miss J Miller
J Miller & C Miller
Adrian Miners
Neil Mitchell
Miss SE Morris
Norma Nichols
Winifred Nightingale
Stuart Orme
Janet & Ted Oselton
Paul Parker
Colin J Parkinson
Trevor Pearce
Bill Peasley
Tom Pentland
Stephen Perry
Photous Photography
Severin Pinder
Mr A Preston
Colin Prosser

Mr & Mrs P Pumprey
Charlotte Purser
Mr & Mrs D Quinn
John & Diane Richardson
Mr & Mrs Geoff & June Ridgway
Jeremy Roberts
Susan Jost Roberts
Ann & Bill Samuel
Peter Sargent
Herbert Saville
Margaret Selves
Geoffrey Severn
RW Shaw (Sleaford)
Cllr John Shearman
    & Mrs Janice Lamplugh
Professor George Shepperson
Pauline Sidebottom
Mr PJ & Mrs MR Simpson
Mr & Mrs CK Skillman
Alan & Shelagh Smith
David & Judith Smith
George Smith
Philip Stafford
Mr & Mrs S Stansfield
Mr & Mrs RW Steward
W J Swann
Grace Taylor
Roger Terrell
John W Thirlwell
Richard & Rosemary Tilson
Glynis & Michael Titman
Malcolm Turner
David Turnock Architects
Des Tuson
Richard N Underwood
University Centre,
    Peterborough
Louis & Linda Verdegem
Vivacity – Culture and Leisure
Margaret Wareing
John & Yvonne Warner
Tom & Angela Watts
Ian Webb
Jill & John Westcombe
Christopher Whitby
Mrs Joyce Wickett
Rohan Wilson
John P Wilkinson
Sylvia & John Woods
His Honour Christopher Young
Valmay Stella Young

Emma Bothamley

Daniela Pierri Brewer

John Clark

Janet Davies

David Good

Richard Houghton

Liz Kemp

Tony Lovell

The Photographers

The Author

Henry Mansell Duckett

Dedication

This book celebrates the 60th anniversary of the founding of Peterborough Civic Society and the 125th anniversary of the creation of Peterborough Photographic Society.

It is dedicated to three people who have made enormous contributions to these societies:

Mr Harry Paten (1901–69)

Founder in 1952 of The Peterborough Society
(later renamed Peterborough Civic Society)

Revd Richard Paten (1932–2012)

Long-time member and active President of Peterborough Civic Society since 1984, Richard's support of the Peterborough in Detail project was a major contribution to its realisation. Sadly he did not live to see its completion.

Mr Peter Harvey

Peter joined Peterborough Photographic Society in 1963, was elected Secretary from 1966 to 1992, was President from 1993 to 1995 and is currently its Treasurer. Peter is an extremely valuable and respected club member who has maintained copious records of PPS for many years with a wealth of information and old documents tracing the Society's history.

Foreword

by Griff Rhys Jones

I think we are a bit lucky here. Lucky to have this book in our hands, lucky that Peterborough has such charms, lucky to be given this astonishing record of such imagination, ingenuity and flair from all ages, and lucky because this book is a ravishing document: a visual cornucopia, a fascinating sourcebook of architectural detail.

As you pore over it, (and I who, shamefully, know little of Peterborough have been stuck to the thing) you will find an audit of the place.

It is irreplaceable stuff. We might be able to reproduce some of these soffit boards, door cases, chimneys, roof gullies or gates. We can admire chimneys, gables or tracery in these pages, but we can never quite replicate the imagination of the people who made them. 'God is in the details', perhaps. If so, for the hundreds of craftsmen, jobbing builders, draftsmen, architects, thatchers, carpenters and householders, all contributing to this overall fabric, God's work was in their hands.

These people were driven by need, economy or the availability of materials. Fashion, invention and whimsy played their part. Utilitarianism may have been an essential driving force. But they represent a historical continuity. Nothing is more essential to the dignity and identity of a city, town or village than its generations of architecture, layout and buildings, both humble and grand. They tell the story. They remind us that we ourselves are not the be all and end all of existence. We are just passing through. There will be others who come after us, others who will not thank us for failing to take care of this modest glory.

Unfortunately, urban landscapes rarely preserve themselves. There is always pressure to change. Inevitable and acceptable as this is, we must always ask exactly what we are doing. Napoleon Bonaparte once described St Mark's Square in Venice as Europe's drawing room, but we could say the same about any town centre. It is our living space and is where we promote comfort, welcome and delight. To smother it with adverts or road signs, to litter the roads with unnecessary garish coloured lines, to bash holes into ancient structures, to allow out-of-scale cheap development is not to bring on the future, it is to ignore the future.

Towns and cities are currently enduring major change. Perhaps we recognise that the motorcar is untenable in city centres. Perhaps we realise that retail may be fading as the internet takes over. High streets are in competition. They have to be safe, but a more vibrant experience than, say, a purpose built shopping centre in order to thrive. We might occupy these drawing rooms for purposes other than shopping; to walk there, attend concerts, to actually live there. We need to preserve, recycle and protect for the future.

If we are to achieve these changes and sustain what we have, then we must know what we've got. Many buildings and building features don't meet national criteria for listing, but nonetheless are important locally to our sense of place. That is especially so in cities such as Peterborough.

So we are lucky that there is a group that keeps watch on this place. That is the Peterborough Civic Society. Together with the Peterborough Photographic Society they have done this painstaking work, not only so that we get something as serious as this book, but also so we get something as fun and entertaining. I salute this. These societies need your support. They need you to join them. At the very least they need you to buy and enjoy this wonderful catalogue of a place. Have fun and be lucky.

Griff Rhys Jones is President of Civic Voice, the national charity for the civic movement in England. It aims to promote civic pride and make places more attractive, enjoyable and distinctive.

Introduction

This book celebrates the built heritage of urban Peterborough and its surrounding villages through photographs of the details of its buildings. We hope that in focussing on specific features instead of general views, we will stimulate surprise, interest and curiosity and contribute to pride in the places that comprise Peterborough. Our aim has been to draw attention to the wealth of building details and ornament that can so easily be overlooked but which can be a source of delight, especially with the benefit of a photographer's sharp eye, zoom lens and perhaps a bit of explanation.

In planning this project we were delighted that Peterborough Photographic Society felt sufficiently enthused to collaborate with us, eight of their members each taking a slice of the area (and two taking to the air to obtain the 'big-detail' aerial pictures).

The pictures were taken with the following guidelines:

- they were only to be taken from public land or land readily accessible to the general public such as footpaths and churchyards.
- external shots only to be taken.
- the subjects must be within Peterborough's Unitary Authority boundary. (We acknowledge that, in error, we strayed over the boundary by a few yards at Alwalton and Norman Cross and trust we have not offended any strongly held civic allegiances!)
- photographers were to look at everything – from the grand to the humble. They were not issued with any list of buildings of architectural or historic interest and were to be guided simply by what caught their attention.

The process produced well over 3,000 pictures. Then, as the text was being written by the Civic Society's Henry Mansell Duckett, more pictures were commissioned to illustrate particular points.

Do we have any conclusions? As Peterborough's ecclesiastical history is so important and the Cathedral and parish churches such rich repositories of detail, we make no apology for their strong presence, although they justify a series of books all to themselves. There are also plenty of examples drawn from houses, be they the grand houses of Burghley and Thorpe Hall or the Victorian semis of central Peterborough.

But Peterborough's roles as a major railway centre, then an engineering centre, in brick-making, publishing and finance have not yielded much striking architectural detail. No doubt this is partly because elaborate detail and ornamentation has long been out of fashion. However, this book proves that there is plenty to celebrate in Peterborough and its villages.

In producing this book we want others to share our pleasure in the buildings of Peterborough and be inspired to cherish and maintain buildings that might otherwise fall into disrepair or be insensitively altered or even destroyed. Perhaps most importantly we want people, Peterborians and visitors alike, to search out and enjoy the city's architectural treasures.

Acknowledgement of the help of those involved is given elsewhere but many others have lent a hand too. We are most grateful – it has been great fun.

Every attempt has been made to be accurate. However if errors are spotted please contact us via the 'Peterborough and its villages in detail' link on the Peterborough Civic Society website homepage: www.peterborough.net/civicsociety.

The Editorial Team

Henry Mansell Duckett
David Jost
Peter Lee
Toby Wood

Note on architectural terms:

Some terms are briefly explained in the course of the text. We hope that the meaning of many others will be self-evident from the images. For readers wishing to consult a glossary, most modern editions in the *Buildings of England* county series now published by Yale University Press carry serviceable glossaries. (A revised volume for Bedfordshire, Huntingdon and Peterborough is currently in preparation). A more detailed source is: Curl, James Stevens, *Oxford Dictionary of Architecture and Landscape Architecture* second edition 2006.

Gateways and Doors

Gateways and doorways may start out as purely functional elements to provide a way in. But the desire to focus attention, welcome (or indeed intimidate) or simply to express social status, tends often to elevate them to the level of a major design opportunity. Image (**3**) opposite is of the gateway from the service yard into the garden of Thorpe Hall. The sunlit garden beckons; this gateway, its door open invitingly, could hardly be more welcoming. Thorpe Hall is arguably the finest of the few comparable houses of the Commonwealth period (1649–60). Peter Mills' design exemplifies perfectly a form of rather homespun Classicism which has acquired the label Artisan Mannerism.

This single gateway is perfectly expressive of the style, is recognised nationally as such, and displays many of its distinctive elements – a heavy, eared door frame with flanking halved pilasters starting out from generous spiralling volutes. The garden into which it beckons is enclosed by its vast encompassing wall constructed, in part, with material salvaged from demolitions that took place within the Cathedral precincts during the Commonwealth. Also pictured is one of the major gates within the great garden wall (**1**), three of which lead out in the cardinal directions into what is left of the parkland; these too are replete with Artisan Mannerist detail and some fine ironwork.

PREVIOUS PAGE

1 Thorpe Hall garden gates

THIS PAGE

2 Thorpe Hall service wing door
3 Thorpe Hall garden door

6

A splendid gateway from Castor with rusticated piers housing tall niches (note the little protective railings) and surmounted by ball finials may also be from the 17th century (**4**), but is of a type which goes on well into the 18th century and beyond. A modern version, finely executed in 18th-century tradition, graces the entrance to Thornhaugh Hall (**5**). Here urns replace the ball finials. Ball finials appear again in Minster Precincts (**6**) and atop a simple but elegant pair of piers within the wall enclosing Walcot Hall's parkland (**7**). Their wide spacing affords a fine view of the 17th- to 18th-century hall itself. At Sutton a garden gate is accompanied by a trio of ball finials of a sort (**8**). But they are not quite spherical and the pair surmounting the gate piers are cupped with acanthus. Moreover they look as though they might be made of terracotta, or possibly of Coade Stone. A charmingly rustic, minimally Classical garden gateway from Alwalton is conveniently dated and carries what are presumably the initials of its original owner (**9**).

PREVIOUS PAGE

4 Castor
5 Thornhaugh
6 Minster
Precincts

THIS PAGE

7 Walcot Hall,
Barnack
8 Sutton
9 Alwalton

8

9

Georgian doorcases of real quality are not plentiful in the area; just a handful of minor examples survive in the city centre itself. Perhaps the best early Georgian doorcase is that from Minster Precincts (**10**), one of a trio of wooden doorcases to a terrace facing the Cathedral's West Front. This short terrace, built in 1728 for Earl Fitzwilliam and quite soon used by the King's School, represents the first appearance in Peterborough of London-type terraced housing. Its doorcases display heavy segmental pediments supported by fluted Doric pilasters.

By far the most sophisticated doorcase – later 18th century – is that which graces the western end of Peterscourt in Midgate (**11**).

It stands within a red-brick porch provided specifically to house it – pickled, as it were, in Gothic Revival aspic. There is nothing at all provincial about this effort with its full entablature, breaking back and forth above an elaborate Gothick fanlight, crowning a Corinthian pilaster order. Indeed this is London work. It was rescued from the London Guildhall, severely damaged in the blitz. The late Frank Perkins (of diesel engine fame) arranged for it to be fixed in the front elevation of Peterscourt in 1953. (It was later re-sited as part of a major restoration of the building). Peterscourt was completed in the 1860s to the designs of Sir George Gilbert Scott – 'Great Scott'. A whole dynasty of Scotts were involved

with the Guildhall until well into the 20th century; it seems unlikely that the Scott connection is entirely coincidental.

The general run of Georgian and later doorcases may just have the simplest pilaster treatment, perhaps a shallow pediment, shell hood or projecting hood supported by shaped brackets, simple fanlight and door with raised and fielded or flush beaded panels. Nonetheless a touch of Renaissance Revival from Wansford manages to run to a pair of Ionic pilasters on each side of the door (**12**).

PREVIOUS PAGE

10 Minster Precincts
11 Peterscourt, Midgate

THIS PAGE

12 Wansford
13 Eye
14 Wansford

THIS PAGE

15 Duke of Bedford cottages, Thorney
16 Glinton

NEXT PAGE

17 Werrington
18 Werrington

Individuality may well be most readily expressed with colour. Strong primary colours are popular, and effective for an individual door. Colour may be supplied too by flanking or surrounding vegetation, often most enjoyable when slightly out of control. Thorney's Bedford Estate housing shows how identical adjoining doors beneath a common pent porch roof may be differentiated simply by adopting contrasting colours for doors and door furniture (**15**). On the other hand, eschewal of colour may be altogether appropriate when it comes to a chaste doorway with surround and keyblock in ashlar masonry (**16**). The same approach adopted at the tiny cottage in Werrington unites door and window in abstract black and white composition beneath a pantiled roof, huge in comparison (**18**).

19

20

21

22

23

24

25

PREVIOUS PAGE

19 Eye
20 Glinton
21 Thorney
22 Northborough
23 Eye
24 Priestgate
25 Stanground

THIS PAGE

26 Wothorpe
27 Thorpe Road
28 Aldermans Drive
29 Deeping Gate
30 Wothorpe

31

32

33

34

35

36

37

38

PREVIOUS PAGE

31 Minster Precincts
32 Cowgate
33 Alwalton
34 Exchange Street
35 Park Road
36 Queen Street

THIS PAGE

37 Thorpe Road
38 Deeping Gate
39 Thorpe Hall
40 Helpston

39

40

41

42

43

44

THIS PAGE

41 Barnack
42 Barnack: St John the Baptist
43 Castor: St Kyneburgha
44 Prior's/Dean's door, Cathedral

Ecclesiastical architecture offers a wide range of doorway and gateway types, the earliest and most rudimentary here being Barnack's pre-Conquest tower door (**41**). Examples from the Cathedral (Prior's or Dean's door – Nave north side) (**44**) and from Barnack's porch (**42**) may appear superficially similar. The arch of the former, framed between shallow Norman buttresses, exhibits well the two species of Norman chevron or zigzag ornament – vertical and horizontal, the latter an early instance at Peterborough. The Barnack doorway is also of three orders of shafts but the Norman capitals have now given way to Early English stiff-leaf, while the arch, though still round (the round form lingers long in the area), has given up chevrons altogether and has instead many fine mouldings. In short,

perhaps only half a century separates these two doorways but we have moved from the Romanesque into the Gothic era.

A chancel doorway from Castor (**43**) is celebrated chiefly for the survival of the inscription surmounting the niche above recording a consecration in 1124. Thorney Abbey's West Front (**45**), as with the rest of the building, is but a tantalising fragment of what once existed. It presents any attempt at analysis with a number of headaches, all manner of changes

having taken place both before and after the Dissolution. 1638 denotes when the monastic remnant was fitted up as the parish church.

THIS PAGE

45 Thorney Abbey

47

Few who enter the Cathedral precincts from Cathedral Square are likely to spot the portcullis groove between the 12th-century Norman Arch of the Great Gate and the superimposed pointed arch of the early 14th-century facade presented to the square (**46**). Inside Minster Precincts, on the north side of Galilee (or Gallery) Court, is the Prior's Gate (**47**), of perhaps a little after 1500. The main arch is four-centred and is bedecked with heraldic and emblematic devices generally intended to be flattering to the Tudors, with a separate opening for pedestrians. It leads through to a complex of buildings of various dates, which has as its core the much restored 13th-century Prior's Lodging. Then, to access the complex (now the Cathedral Chapter House

PREVIOUS PAGE

46 The Great Gate,
Cathedral Square
47 Prior's Gate, Minster Precincts
48 Minster Precincts

THIS PAGE

49 Bottle Lodges,
Burghley House
50 Alwalton
51 Orton Hall

and offices), a Victorian Gothic Revival porch and lobby have been cleverly fitted into the angle (**48**).

The spectacular gateway to Burghley's parkland from the west, the so-called Bottle Lodges (**49**), is quite some distance – about a mile, 'over hill, over dale' – from the great house. Built as late as 1801 to the designs of the Stamford architect WD Legg, the gateway manages to display just about all the detailed elements and motifs familiar from the house. A triumphal arch theme, Tuscan columns, octagonal turrets, niches, obelisk finials – in short, the whole Elizabethan-Jacobean repertoire – is skilfully reassembled and revived.

Genuinely Jacobean, though not *in situ*, is the porch from Alwalton (**50**). This entrance frontispiece – Ionic columns superimposed above Tuscan – started out as part of nearby Chesterton, the Dryden family mansion, demolished in the early 19th century. Other salvaged and recycled bits of Chesterton are to be found in the locality. From Orton Hall a set of double doors, panelled overall in a mid 19th-century version of linenfold, stands beneath a four-centred arch (**51**). The whole arrangement is beautifully detailed, even if the stonework – bands of ashlar alternating with rock-faced stone in narrower courses – is somewhat forbidding.

Boot-scrapers

These once essential features of civilised urban and rural living now tend to be overlooked and generally disregarded, rusting away or nestling, half-hidden, amidst the vegetation at the foot of a wall (**1**). Yet they do still survive in surprising numbers, if not always in the best condition. The occupants of the prestigious five-bay house in Priestgate (**2**) would doubtless have arrived home having waded through the organic detritus and equine fall-out of the Marketstead, now Cathedral Square. When, in the mid 19th century, the house was expensively refronted with ashlar masonry, provision was made for recessed boot scrapers of standard cast iron pattern to be slotted alongside the pilaster bases on either side of the fine doorway.

An elegant modern example, in wrought iron it seems, is from Alwalton (**3**); handy, say, following a Sunday afternoon walk to Castor

THIS PAGE

1 Eye

across the Nene water meadows. Churches too needed their boot scrapers. These seem often to have survived in better maintained condition than domestic examples. The local blacksmith would have been adept at knocking up a wrought iron set for the village church which was simple, functional, relatively inexpensive, yet in keeping. That at Bainton (**4**) has lost a couple of trefoiled finials to poorly aimed boots, though one survives to express its Gothic credentials.

THIS PAGE

2 Priestgate
3 Alwalton
4 Bainton: St Mary

Most urban examples, whether free-standing or recessed, tend to be in cast iron; mostly off-the-peg items attempting to pick up on architectural themes then current, whether Classical, Gothic or something in between. The recess in the example from Russell Street is pointed (**5**), as befits a gabled terrace fronting directly onto the pavement. By contrast the splendid free-standing pair of addorsed (back to back, as opposed to affronted) mythical winged beasts (gryphons?) (**6**) seems rather superior to something merely off-the-peg, (though the number stamped on the casting suggests that at least 410 were made). Perhaps this was a bespoke design deemed fit to grace the Duke of Bedford's Thorney estate housing and related structures, much of which was executed to the designs of 'Rogue Goth' architect SS Teulon.

7

PREVIOUS PAGE

5 Russell Street
6 Thorney
7 Thorney Abbey

THIS PAGE

8 Barnack: St John the Baptist
9 Wothorpe
10 Orton Hall
11 Sutton

Steeples, Towers, Turrets and Cupolas

We are concerned here with features ranging from steeples to weather vanes – in short, anything which scratches the sky.

Peterborough Cathedral's majestic scale exerts a considerable presence upon the city. An aerial view from the south-west (**1**) shows its immediate environs still crowded with the substantial remnants of former monastic buildings, many adapted to modern usage. At close quarters the Cathedral's chief 'wow-factor' comes from a sudden appreciation of its unique Gothic portico West Front. The organisation of this extraordinary screen façade, as well as possible sources of influence, may perplex art historians but its impact is undeniably dramatic. So far as making an outstanding impact upon the skyline is concerned, Peterborough's Cathedral lacks the advantages of many. An assortment of structural

THIS PAGE

1 Peterborough Cathedral

THIS PAGE

2 Burghley House
3 Burghley House
4 Wothorpe Lodge

mishaps over the centuries has deprived the great Romanesque-into-Gothic structure of a really strong vertical accent. Yet a silhouette bristling with spirelets, pinnacles, turrets and gables coalesces with towers left unfinished or truncated to produce a distinctive skyline all of its own.

The role of the Cecils of Burghley House, particularly that of William, Lord Burghley, its builder, in the affairs of State and Court looms large in the history of Elizabethan England. Burghley is a prime example of an Elizabethan/Jacobean 'Prodigy House' – in short prodigiously large, showy and expressive of high status. Burghley's fantastical skyline – an extraordinary confection of spires, finials, turrets and chimneys, the latter masquerading as clusters of Tuscan columns – is unforgettable (**2** and **3**).

A mile or so away to the west at Wothorpe, in the very corner of our area, is the now ruined Wothorpe Lodge (**4**). It is a remarkable progeny of Burghley if utterly different in form, style and function. Its square plan, with four towers turning octagonal at the top, presents a distinctively compact composition – the upper parts of the towers enlivened by Italian Mannerist flourishes. Wothorpe Lodge was built early in the 17th century for William Cecil's son Thomas, 1st Earl of Exeter, ostensibly, according to a near contemporary, 'to retire to out of the dust while his great house of Burghley was a-sweeping'. One modern commentator though has mischievously described Wothorpe in rather less prosaic terms as a 'Nooky Palace'!

5

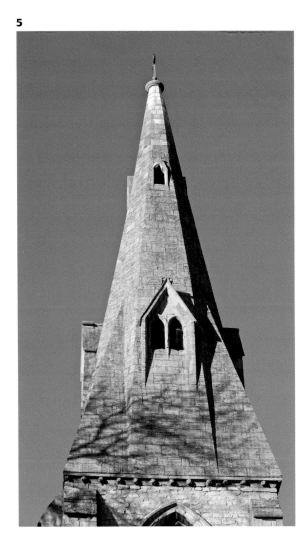

6

7

8

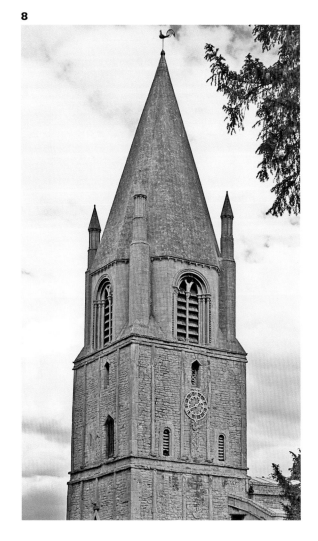

Many of Peterborough's church spires would not look out of place along the Nene Valley west of the city. Fletton (**5**), Stanground (**6**) and Paston for example: are broach spires of the late 13th century. (The term broach refers to the pyramidal features at the base of a spire, which effect the steeple's transition from square to octagonal form.) Most too are provided with two tiers of lucarnes (gabled openings within spires) such as those from Bainton's later steeple (**7**).

Barnack's steeple (**8**) is celebrated nationally, and not only for its remarkable Late Saxon tower. The squat early 13th-century octagonal spire which crowns the tower – tall pinnacles sitting upon small very low broaches – is one of the earliest in the country. Helpston's steeple (**9**), considerably later and rebuilt, also turns octagonal low down and is surmounted by a very short spire. Spires would soon become taller and more slender in the two centuries which followed, culminating in the veritable needles of the 15th century. Several of the group are recognisable by their form or detail. Glinton's steeple (**10**), looking alarmingly tall and narrow in long views, is further distinguishable due to its entasis, or curvature, an optical correction more familiar from Classical architecture. Stanground and Fletton, whilst close neighbours, are immediately separable since the capstones to Stanground's 'pencil' spire are blackened. (This could be due to a repair in sandstone weathering quite differently.) At Eye (**11**), in the Fen proper, the 19th-century church steeple was once surmounted by a broach spire, which had to be taken down in the 1980s as it was unsafe. The saddleback tower cap seen today was its replacement.

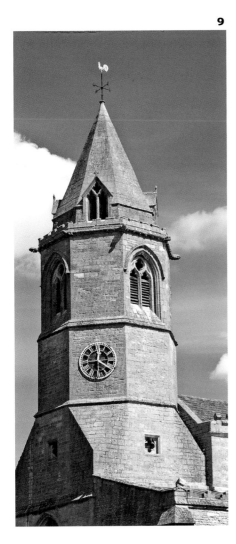

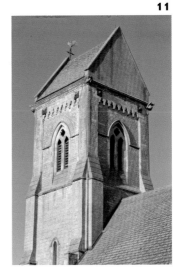

12   14

The noble 15th-century tower of St John's in Cathedral Square (**12**) (which once carried a needle spire, presumably of lead-clad timber) may now happily be seen to advantage from all angles, having been freed from the unwelcome close attentions of the former Norwich Union Building. A couple of medieval-looking spires punctuate the city centre skyline to complement the spirelets and pinnacles of the Cathedral's West Front. However, in fact they are both 19th century. St Mark's Church (**13**) in Lincoln Road is Gothic Revival and possessed of much originality. The spire of the former Trinity Presbyterian Church (**14**) in Priestgate, also mid19th-century, closes the view along Cross Street. It sits on top of a fine Classical tower stage with a full complement of pilasters, pediments and so on. The whole ensemble is a mixture of Gothic and Classical modes.

PREVIOUS PAGE

5   Fletton: St Margaret
6   Stanground: St John the Baptist
7   Bainton: St Mary
8   Barnack: St John the Baptist

THIS PAGE

9   Helpston: St Botolph
10   Glinton: St Benedict
11   Eye: St Matthew
12   Cathedral Square, St John the Baptist
13   Lincoln Road: St Mark
14   Priestgate

16

18

Peterborough's largely uneventful surburban townscape was suddenly enlivened in the late 20th century at Netherton by a rather surprising intruder (**15**). This sinuous brick bell tower of St Jude's Church, by Peterborough architect Joseph Robotham, evokes something of the spirit of the free compositional forms of the 19th- to 20th-century Catalan architect Antonio Gaudi, and is an arresting structure.

An equally flat topography characterises the northern approach into the city by rail. Here the first significant vertical feature is provided by the characteristic forms and colours of the slender minarets and domes of two mosques (**16**).

Approaching Peterborough from the south, through Hampton, the eye is drawn to the huge ogee-capped feature atop the Serpentine Green shopping mall (**17**), a genuine lantern, lighting the central space beneath.

A host of minor sky-scratching accents are scattered throughout the city centre and beyond. Fine cupolas crown a bank in Cathedral Square (**18**) and the Town Hall (**19**) above its portico. Atop the Customs House (**20**) is a dainty lantern; the cylinder at the base of its weathervane is said to contain a time capsule. Park Road Baptist Church (**21**) sports a cupola-cum-lantern (housing a ventilator it seems) which exudes faint

24

25

Arts and Crafts touches. Around the Burghley Square junction are clustered a number of turrets and the like which lend a baronial touch, including a candle-snuffer roof, nicely slated, to a polygonal window bay in Broadway (**22**). A pretty open cupola with ogival cap and weathervane (**23**) graces the skyline of Orton Longueville. At Ufford a particularly dainty pyramidal dovecote cap to a pyramidal roof just about manages to scratch the sky (**24**), whereas from the exotic skyline of Burghley (**25**) a host of assertive ogee-capped turrets proudly wave their heraldic weathervanes.

PREVIOUS PAGE

15 Netherton: St Jude
16 Gladstone Street
17 Serpentine Green
18 Cathedral Square
19 Town Hall, Bridge Street

THIS PAGE

20 The Customs House,
    Town Bridge
21 Park Road
22 Broadway
23 Orton Longueville
24 Ufford
25 Burghley

26

27

28

29

30

31

THIS PAGE

26 Westgate
27 Long Causeway
28 Minster Precincts
29 Orton Hall
30 Cathedral Square:
    St John the Baptist
31 Thorpe Road

NEXT PAGE

32 Thorney Abbey
33 Barnack
34 Longthorpe
35 Longthorpe Tower

More of the same, or similar, from Westgate (**26**), Long Causeway (**27**) and Minster Precincts (**28**) – the late 13th-century Abbot's Gate. The example from Long Causeway, its unusually shaped ogival copper cap crowning a tourelle above a cornice corbelled out in the form of false machicolations, must be by the same architect as a near identically detailed building in London's Oxford Street, though there the tourelle has now lost its cap. A slender turret of nicely variegated stonework crowned with a frilly openwork parapet adorns Orton Hall (**29**). Yet more slender, a pinnacle from the splendid porch of St John's in the city centre (**30**). Panelled, crocketed and showing evidence of recent stonework repair, a pinnacle such as this, while resembling a mere decorative flourish, is also functional, adding vertical load

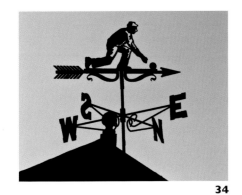

to counter a lateral thrust. By no means slender is the thumping superstructure of the gatehouse to the former Sessions House in Thorpe Road (**31**), replete with turrets adorned with false machicolations, arrow-loops and the like. William Donthorne's beautifully executed pile, resembling in this view some mighty medieval castle keep, is a splendid example of the Norman style as it was briefly revived around the 1840s.

Weathervanes, high up, present fewer constraints to the designer. Their traditional function will often have been overtaken by personal flights of fancy or humour. Those atop church spires and towers will usually be predictable, as with the heraldic banner from Thorney Abbey (**32**). Birds feature frequently, particularly the weathercock. At Barnack (**33**) the birds of the air hitch a lift on the splendid tail of a spinningly unconcerned cockerel. Domestic flights of fancy may throw up the whimsical, though trumpeting angels, coach and horses and witches riding broomsticks, etc., all cut an arresting silhouette against the sky. Racing greyhounds, prancing horses and the like will probably indicate the interests of the building's owner, and we are left in no doubt as to the nature of the sporting activity being celebrated at Longthorpe (**34**).

An appropriate tailpiece for this section is perhaps Peterborough's most celebrated tower – Longthorpe (**35**) – with its early 14th-century domestic wall paintings of at least national significance. Externally it most resembles a Northumbrian pele tower, slipped south.

Gables and Pediments

THIS PAGE

1   Cathedral Square/Bridge Street

NEXT PAGE

2   Bridge Street
3   St Peter's Road
4   Bridge Street: Town Hall

Gables and pediments share a similar function; namely to close the ends of a pitched roof. What distinguishes them is the manner in which this is achieved. Gables, atop gable-end walls, may be triangular, following the slopes of a roof, but may also adopt other configurations (shaped, crow-stepped, Dutch, etc.,) to create in effect a parapet which partly disguises the roof form. If triangular, the gable might be finished with an unadorned verge or have bargeboards to provide a decorative treatment to cover it. Pediments on the other hand originated with the triangular gables following the roof slopes above the portico colonnades or facades of Classical temples. They came to adorn subordinate features of all kinds and may be segmental or triangular; each has many variants: open or broken-top, broken-base or open-bed, scrolled, etc.

3

4

Two pediments nod to each other across Bridge Street. That of the Town Hall's noble portico (executed in Hollington stone, a sandstone from Staffordshire, rather than a local limestone; though other stone dressings are in Clipsham limestone) is supported by a giant order of Corinthian columns, its tympanum sporting a cartouche with the arms of the city (**4**). Almost opposite, another Neo-Georgian pediment surmounts not a portico but a three bay projection in the façade (**2**). In the pediment here the cartouche, conveniently dated, is accompanied by lavish swags – festoons of flowers, fruit and vegetables, etc., while the modillions (repeated brackets) have acanthus decoration to their undersides. The image demonstrates the quality of workmanship in brick and stone often achieved during the inter-war period. Fine brickwork in English bond (alternate courses of headers and stretchers) complements the Classically derived stonework executed in what appears to be Portland stone.

The rear Town Hall entrance bay is distinguished by a pilaster order (a fanciful variant of the Ionic which seems to be of architect Berry Webber's own devising) supporting a plain pediment in front of a blind attic storey (**3**), all this in nicely contrasting red and grey bricks with stone dressings.

7

In Priestgate a simple, shallow pediment, as befits the severity of the fluted Greek Doric colonnade to the portico beneath, surmounts the entrance bay of the Museum (**5**). The ashlar masonry here, regularly coursed and in fairly small blocks, suggests from its buff and pinkish hues that it is the famed Ketton freestone, with which many of Cambridge's colleges were faced for about two centuries from the end of the 17th century.

In Cathedral Square, facing north, is the shaped gable to the return elevation of Palmer and Holden's former National Provincial Bank of 1928–29 (**6**), arguably the finest provincial bank building of its time in the country. (The elaborate lamp standard in the foreground, one of only three to survive,

celebrates the introduction of electric street lighting to the city in 1903. It has been much moved about and was originally in the Stanley Road Recreation Ground.) The gable to the bank's main entrance (**1**) is something to behold. The inspiration for this *tour de force* was Kirby Hall in Northamptonshire. The gable itself is crowded with motifs, whilst the fanciful giant Ionic pilaster order below reflects something of Kirby Hall's borrowed French Renaissance flavour.

In Church Street a 19th-century shaped gable, with crowning chimney stack, (**7**) lords it over a couple of plain gables to the staggered frontages of much earlier buildings.

From Alwalton comes a shaped gable with the kind of simple geometric devices familiar from much Elizabethan display (**8**).

PREVIOUS PAGE
5 Priestgate
6 Cathedral Square/Bridge Street
7 Church Street

THIS PAGE
8 Alwalton
9 Broadway
10 Long Causeway

9

Very different is the shallow brick crow-stepped gable – probably late 19th/early 20th century – which makes an appearance both towards Broadway and Stanley Road (**9**). To the east side of Long Causeway the skyline is adorned with a splendid trio of gables of broadly Dutch type, brick with stone dressings, and sporting generous volutes, crowning pediments and a profusion of urn finials (**10**). The whole ensemble, together with two tall accompanying chimney stacks, has something of a Mannerist air about it. Mannerism with knobs on!

12

THIS PAGE

11 Glinton Manor
12 Glinton Manor
13 Thorpe Hall: Service wing

NEXT PAGE

14 Thorpe Hall:
Garden feature

Glinton Manor's Jacobean/Early Stuart gables adopt varied ogee shapes of different sizes, the larger of the two shown here (**11**) with an oculus window at the summit, the smaller pinched in at the base to impart a bulbous form (**12**). Both carry little ball finials to the shoulder or kneeler stones at the springing of their curves.

From Thorpe Hall a couple of gables which might be described as Dutch, save that the way in which the generous volutes are handled on the service wing (**13**) speaks more of the Artisan Mannerism for which the building is famed. The second gable (**14**), now a garden feature on its east-west axis, originated as the entrance frontispiece to a lost wing. Sporting a large crowning segmental pediment and three oculi, it lay until

comparatively recently flat on its face in the grass. The vogue for this type of 'Artisan' gable seems to have taken off nationally around 1620 after the mason/architect John Smythson (one of a dynasty) had made a drawing (which survives) of 'My Ladye Cooke's House' in Holborn, London. Hence 'Holborn' gable as an alternative term for this type.

15

16

17

18

THIS PAGE

15 Cowgate
16 Cross Street
17 Park Road
18 Cathedral Square

NEXT PAGE

19 Park Road
20 Park Road
21 Broadway
22 Broadway

The Victorians were adept at playing all manner of games with shaped gables and pediments, borrowing promiscuously from any style which suited. One such gable from what is now a pub in Cowgate is proudly dated (**15**). Another, not far away, facing into Cross Street rises above a substantial cornice only loosely connected with Classical precedent (**16**). The flank of Westgate House running north from Westgate displays an extraordinary phalanx of inventive forms. Beginning with a wide segmental, broken-base pediment (**17**), its tympanum with pilasters carried through and a window head with swags festooned from its keystone, the procession carries on with about a dozen variants on the shaped gable theme (**19** and **20**).

A pediment-cum-gable in Cathedral Square (**18**) is odd in several respects. Equilateral triangle in shape, its brick filled tympanum looks uncomfortably random surmounting the stone-faced storey beneath – the more so when one appreciates that the storey below that, with shallow bow windows, is again in brick. Side by side in Broadway are two ranges of building each employing the pediment to define a pair of pavilions at their extremities. The first, in stone, has open-bed pediments supported by rusticated pilasters and, somewhat surprisingly, a rusticated arch with keystone rising into the tympana (**21**). To its immediate north is a range where the terminal pavilions are capped with equilateral triangled pediments-cum-gables, their cornices of wood, above diminutive 'Venetian' windows (**22**).

PETERBOROUGH and its villages IN DETAIL

23

24

25

26

THIS PAGE

23 Park Road
24 Park Road
25 Broadway
26 Burghley Road
27 Park Road

NEXT PAGE

28 Manor House
     Street
29 Fletton
30 Lincoln Road
31 Lincoln Road
32 Lincoln Road
33 Park Road

27

Victorian domestic expansion north and south of the city produced just about every permutation on gable form and decoration which it is possible to imagine. Chequer-work in brick and stone, a plethora of patterns in *faux* timber-framing, around Lincoln Road, Park Road and their tributaries, much play with panels of knapped flint, even some sculpted brick and terracotta. Several of the ventures into black and white place a gable awkwardly, if picturesquely, above a canted brick bay (**25**), necessitating the introduction of corner struts supported in stone corbels. The example illustrated also shows the form of sash window, popular around 1900, where only the upper sash is multi-paned. A better example perhaps may be seen in the section on windows (page 65, number **61**).

28

29

30

31

32

33

36

37

38

THIS PAGE

34 Bridge Street
35 Cathedral Square
36 Park Road
37 Burghley Road
38 Burghley Road

NEXT PAGE

39 Broadway
40 Broadway
41 North of Westwood
    Road bridge

A similarly rich profusion exists when it comes to decorative bargeboards employed to hide the gable verge. It is probably safe to say that no medieval examples survive, at least in the urban area. However, in Bridge Street (at the former Bull and Dolphin) three projecting gables (two are shown) carry quite respectable reproductions (**34**). It is doubtful whether any of the exposed timbers visible on the front of this building have much of a structural function (though they may cover some original timbers in replica) despite the fact that behind this front lies the substantial remnant of a possibly 16th-century timber-framed structure.

Rather more fanciful bargeboards, carrying decoration suggestive of strapwork, and with crowning finials with drops beneath, adorn this very enjoyable piece of pastiche (**35**) in

Cathedral Square (listed, but 'solely as a curiosity'). Built in 1911, it is one of several similar buildings commissioned by Jesse Boot, of Boots the Chemist fame. Others are in Bury St Edmunds and Derby, and all display a profusion of Elizabethan/Jacobean/Stuart decoration in timber and plasterwork pargetting, and sport carved figures of local historical import. The Derby building was designed for Boot by Morley Horder; much about the detailing as well as the general conception suggests that Horder could well have been Boot's architect here too.

In Burghley Road elaborate bargeboards grace a couple of serious attempts at 'Tudorbethan' or 'Free-Tudor' style, both nicely detailed and with either plaster infill or brick nogging to the panels between the timbers (**37** and **38**).

Even the Eastfield signal box (**41**), built in 1894 for the Great Northern Railway, is permitted a fancy bargeboard. The classic mechanical signal box was developed in the 1870s and 80s. About 500 mechanical boxes survive – about 10% of those operating in 1960 – but with Network Rail proposing to concentrate all of its signalling control into fourteen national centres it would seem that only those outside the Network Rail system can have a long-term future.

1

Windows

This section runs the whole gamut of the forms of aperture through which light, and where appropriate air, is admitted to buildings. The breadth of examples from the area is extraordinary, ranging from the rudimentary triangular-headed early 11th-century window opening on Barnack's church tower (**2**) or the even simpler little aperture – reset – at Woodston Church (**3**), through the windows that create the more regularly proportioned elevations of Georgian and Victorian buildings (**5**), to the cliffs of minimally detailed modern curtain walling in the city centre (**1**).

The only Norman windows in their original form (save for the addition of glazing) surviving at the Cathedral are those high on

THIS PAGE

1 Westgate

2

3

4

THIS PAGE

2 Barnack: St John the Baptist
3 Woodston: St Augustine
4 Cathedral: North Transept
5 Exchange Street/Cathedral Square
6 Cathedral: North Presbytery aisle
7 Burghley House

5

6

7

the east elevation of the North Transept (**4**). These remain in their original state simply because, until the Civil War period, a large Lady Chapel abutted – see the outline of its gable over – and so no reason was seen to enlarge the glazed area, or to introduce tracery. A little further east along the north side is a Norman window (chevrons and billet mouldings to the arch over) essentially retaining its original form but with the addition of 15th-century tracery (**6**). The latter now holds Victorian stained glass (by William Wailes of Newcastle) which borrowed light from within permits us to enjoy. When the balance of light is in the opposite direction

Wailes's strong primary colours are cast onto the burial place of Katharine of Aragon.

Skipping nimbly over the three centuries or so that witnessed the development of tracery, to arrive in the later Tudor period, we arrive in the era when some great 'prodigy houses' could be characterised as resembling 'more glass than wall'. Ample demonstration of these vast expanses of mullioned and transomed fenestration is available both at Burghley House (**7**) and Milton Hall. A number of the smaller scale manor houses or houses of the yeomanry in the area reflect these details, albeit in a more restrained fashion (e.g. **13** and **15** overleaf).

8

9

10

11

12

Typical of the modest mullioned windows of the area is that from Northborough (**8**); a simple three-light window – one opening casement and two fixed deadlights. The lights are separated by ovolo-moulded mullions and there is a hood mould above – this is a Classical *cyma recta* (a *cyma reversa* would have an opposing S-shaped curvature). In another three-light window, from Glinton (**10**), where sliding sashes have now replaced casements, the mullions are simply chamfered (and on plan diamond shaped). Projecting bays, usually canted as at Wansford (**13**), commonly have wide mullioned windows wrapping around the whole bay. At Marholm (**14**), in a house dated 1633, a pair of two-light mullioned windows, the lower adapted to receive sliding sashes, are graced with dainty Classical pediments, segmental above triangular.

Larger windows, with the addition of a transom (a horizontal bar of the same moulded cross-section dividing the window into two or more lights in height) such as that from Alwalton (**12**) – both mullions and transoms ovolo-moulded in section – also survive in considerable numbers.

PREVIOUS PAGE

8   Northborough Manor
9   Orton Waterville
10 Glinton
11 Alwalton
12 Alwalton

THIS PAGE

13 Wansford
14 Marholm
15 Wothorpe
16 Priestgate

20

THIS PAGE

17 Thorpe Hall west front
18 Thorpe Hall east front
19 Lincoln Road
20 Park Road

An assortment of mullioned and transomed windows occupy two of the main elevations – west and east – of Thorpe Hall (**17** and **18**). One of the extraordinary aspects of the fenestration of the great house is the diversity of its treatment between elevations. Windows to north and south are organised in fairly standard form; square and rectangular openings, hierarchically arranged and, most probably, originally cross mullioned and transomed. However, the central part of the west elevation is lit by large mullioned and transomed windows which would not look amiss on an Elizabethan 'prodigy house'. To the east the windows are quite different again, arranged in three bays in tripartite form and all rising through the two main storeys. The outer bays project slightly, while all three deploy permutations on the 'Venetian window' motif with an arched centre light. It was long assumed that Thorpe Hall's east elevation had been significantly tampered with in the 19th century, but this is now considered unlikely. A late 19th-century bay window in Lincoln Road (**19**) looks as though it may have been inspired by this east elevation.

By the 19th century the mullioned and transomed form had become particularly useful, not only for domestic buildings grand or otherwise, but also for a whole range of commercial and institutional buildings where large expanses of glazing were required. The Park Road elevation of Westgate House (**20**) presents a long procession of such windows beneath about a dozen varied fancy gables, all redolent of a Jacobean ensemble, but executed in red pressed brick with stone dressings.

Thorney's Tank Yard buildings of 1855 (**21**) exploit the mullioned and transomed form in an assortment of shapes, sizes and tiers of lights, most with the cast iron lattice characteristic of the Bedford Estate work in the village (**22**). Grander houses occasionally presented an opportunity for considerable liberties to be taken with the form, as with this highly original piece of Victorian design from Wothorpe (**23**) – probably the work of Edward Browning the architect, as his own residence.

The windows with mullioned and transomed crosses to both storeys of the former Wortley's Almshouses (**24**), now pub, appear from the arrangement of their stone reveals to have been enlarged. The openings seem originally to have been roughly square, and could have held two-light casements or even sashes. Built in 1744, through the munificence of Edward Wortley Montagu MP, as a workhouse, the building became an almshouse in 1837 following plans to provide a new workhouse in Thorpe Road, receiving in the process the extensive 'Tudorising' makeover which imparts its present character.

THIS PAGE

21 Thorney
22 Thorney
23 Wothorpe
24 Westgate

25

26

27

28

29

30

31

32

PREVIOUS PAGE

25 Orton Longueville
26 Orton Longueville
27 Eye
28 Thorney
29 Werrington
30 Long Causeway
31 Helpston
32 Barnack

THIS PAGE

33 Barnack
34 Thorney
35 Thorney

A casement – essentially a metal or timber frame holding a hinged light as opposed to lights within sliding sashes or pivot-hung – may take many forms. An almost random sample is shown here. Often it will be the pattern of leading, holding individual pieces of glass in lead cames, which catches the eye. Latticed patterns in squares or diamond shaped lozenges predominate, but with variations. Sometimes bits of coloured glass are incorporated; heraldic devices, say, as in the Ortons (**26**), or the red lion announcing the dedication of the pub in Eye (**27**). Several cottages in Barnack catch the eye, their simple casements aggrandised, as it were, by a random juxtaposition of bits of architectural salvage of late medieval origin (**32** and **33**).

Thorney's cast iron latticed casements, which survive in considerable numbers, are striking whether painted black (**28**) or white (**34**). Set for the most part within chamfered reveals, they come with a variety of detail to the window head above. Some have flat brick arches in a contrasting brick, while others are graced by composite lintels, partly in brick but supported by large stone shoulder-pieces sporting fancy profiles. Similarly idiosyncratic moulding profiles frame the windows of a surviving contemporary shopfront in the same village (**35**).

36

37

38

39

40

41

THIS PAGE

36 Minster Precincts
37 Minster Precincts
38 Minster Precincts
39 Priestgate
40 Peakirk
41 Minster Precincts

The sash window – essentially a rebated frame with one or more panes of glass forming a single light set within a larger frame – takes a number of forms. Opening sashes may slide vertically – the most common form – or horizontally. The latter are known as Yorkshire sliding-sashes; two examples survive, side by side, in Minster Precincts (**36** and **37**). The vertically sliding sash is a hung sash, suspended by cords or chains from pulleys within the box frame. It may be single-hung if one sash only moves or, if both can be moved, double-hung.

The boxed sliding or double-hung sash window, which was to play such an important role in the architecture of the Georgian era in particular, seems to have been first introduced in the 1670s or 1680s. Whether introduced from the Netherlands (particularly influential at the time) or an English invention is a matter of debate. By Queen Anne's reign the vertically sliding sash had become generally popular, quickly displacing the 18th-century casement.

The London Building Acts of 1707 and 1709 had made attacks on exposed woodwork since the memory of the Great Fire was still relatively fresh. So the box frame, at first virtually in the same plane as the wall, receded about four inches into the reveal. This stage of development may be seen in examples from Minster Precincts (**38**) and Priestgate (**39**) both within plain stone architraves. An Act of 1774 further banished the box frame, consigning it to a rebate in

the window reveal so as to leave only a narrow strip of woodwork visible, as at Peakirk (**40**) where the stone architrave is moulded.

Precisely how long these developments took to trickle down to the provinces is often difficult to determine, but similar progressions can be traced in the area during the 18th century. Earlier double-hung sashes, such as the example from Minster Precincts (**41**) (where the uneven reflections indicate the retention of some old crown glass), tend also to be subdivided by rather fat, somewhat obtrusive glazing-bars (astragals) between the panes. The astragals tend to become thinner as the century progresses, acquiring ever more refined moulding profiles, contributing to the slender elegance of Late Georgian proportion.

THIS PAGE
42 Eye
43 Eye
44 Priestgate
45 Thorney

The elegant balance of Georgian sash windows within a façade may seem to have been achieved without effort. In reality, more often than not, it was controlled by carefully applied rules of proportion. Prominent amongst these when it came to the relative size and shape of window apertures was a deployment of the ratio 1:√2; that is the ratio of the side of a square to its diagonal. A larger square taking the diagonal of the smaller as its side will be double its area. Known and used in antiquity, transmitted to the Middle Ages (its use has been well attested in the development of plans of the greater churches) and rediscovered by the Renaissance, it continues to have currency and utility in design. The 1:√2 ratio is that of a piece of A4 paper, or indeed the face of the dust jacket to this book with the flap opened out.

The organization of windows to the great Palladian houses or Georgian terraces of cities like London, Bath or Liverpool, will typically exhibit a sequence of window proportions, top down, of 1x1 (three panes over three) 1x√2 (three over six) or 1x√3 (six over six) and 1x2 (six over nine). The full sequence is difficult to demonstrate clearly with accessible examples from our area but, taking the classic Georgian sash window generally found in the area (the quartet from Norman House Norman Cross [**46**],

PREVIOUS PAGE

46 Norman Cross
47 Westgate

THIS PAGE

48 Peakirk
49 Queen Street
50 Hampton

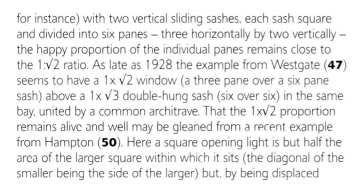

for instance) with two vertical sliding sashes, each sash square and divided into six panes – three horizontally by two vertically – the happy proportion of the individual panes remains close to the 1:√2 ratio. As late as 1928 the example from Westgate (**47**) seems to have a 1x √2 window (a three pane over a six pane sash) above a 1x √3 double-hung sash (six over six) in the same bay, united by a common architrave. That the 1x√2 proportion remains alive and well may be gleaned from a recent example from Hampton (**50**). Here a square opening light is but half the area of the larger square within which it sits (the diagonal of the smaller being the side of the larger) but, by being displaced

asymmetrically, an elegant arrangement of fixed margin-lights is produced.

Two examples are offered (**48** and **49**) of that Georgian favourite, known variously as the 'Venetian' window, the 'Palladian' window (Andea Palladio, Italian architect: 1508–80) or 'Serliana' (Sebastiano Serlio, Italian theorist: 1475–1554). Tripartite in form with an arched central opening, it was employed extensively throughout the period when the Classical language of architecture held sway, often to impart a central emphasis and symmetry.

THIS PAGE

51 Minster Precincts
52 Minster Precincts
53 Barnack
54 Park Road
55 Werrington
56 Priestgate
57 Cowgate

NEXT PAGE

58 Bridge Street
59 Lincoln Road
60 Alwalton
61 Fletton
62 Cowgate

Earlier Georgian window heads may be formed as segmental rather than flat brick arches. A couple of examples from Minster Precincts (**51** and **52**) show firstly the meticulously fine brickwork involved in forming such an arch with voussoirs of fine red rubbers (a soft brick, sawn then rubbed to precise shape) with the thinnest of joints run in a lime-putty rather than mortar. Secondly, from an adjacent window, we may appreciate the difficulty faced today when attempting a seemly repair to a slipped voussoir (**52**).

Window proportions had begun to change in the 18th century, particularly with the advent of Neoclassicism. By the first decades of the 19th century window apertures, which hitherto had usually

been tall and narrow, tended to become wider in proportion to height. A Regency house in Barnack (**53**) demonstrates the change in aesthetic; the sashes now have eight over eight panes. Heavily rusticated to architrave and lintel, the windows to this house also illustrate the widespread use by builders and craftsmen of pattern books in order to impart a little Classical detail here and there. Pattern books had become widely available by the end of the 18th century with the result that at this period the overlap between 'vernacular' and 'polite' architecture was probably at its greatest.

The gradual breakdown of stricter Georgian proportion also made possible the introduction of an assortment of tripartite forms – wide double-hung sashes with flanking half-sashes, margin-lights and margin-panes often with coloured glass, and so forth. A tendency towards more and larger windows, encouraged by the repeal of window tax in 1851, finally removed just about all earlier design constraints. Thus was opened, in the heat and energy generated by the Victorian 'Battle of the Styles', a veritable Pandora's box of period detail, often incongruously if enjoyably applied.

65

67

THIS PAGE

63 City Road
64 Town Hall, Bridge Street
65 Long Causeway
66 Lincoln Road
67 Town Hall, St Peter's Road

This rich eclectic mix continued well into the 20th century until it was calmed, to some degree, by the eventual arrival in this country of Modernism. The dictum 'form follows function' became a rallying cry. Eventually glass curtain walling, sheer, faceted or in receding planes, often came to determine the very form (**63**). Along the way the so-called Free styles attempted a further eclectic mingling, as with E Berry Webber's Town Hall, completed in 1933 in what used, somewhat disparagingly, to be termed a Free 'Wrenaisance' style. He found it possible nonetheless to run to a derivative of the Diocletian window (**64**) at the ends of its wings. A projecting bay in Lincoln Road (**66**) – in effect a flattened bow – has mullioned and transomed windows with, in the lower storey, a tripartite arched form deriving from the so-called 'Ipswich' window, itself deriving from the Venetian window.

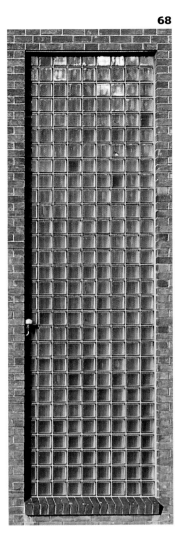

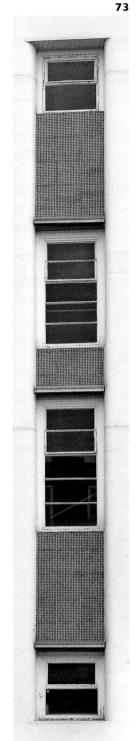

70   72

Other manifestations of Neo-Georgian taste – expanses of repeated sash windows – could be given interest and symmetry by means of a columned or pilastered architectural frame (an aedicule) to a central bay, as with the example dated 1931 from Long Causeway (**65**). A little before this the Steel Windows Association had begun to promote new developments in steel window production. By the 1950s Crittall had become synonymous with the 20th-century metal window, accounting for nearly half total production. Very many steel windows, both commercial and domestic, have now given way to UPVC, but the distinctive curved forms and horizontal proportions of those lighting the bays of a double-fronted house in Maxey survive as a good example (**69**).

THIS PAGE

68 Bridge Street
69 Maxey
70 Serpentine Green, Hampton
71 Town Hall, Bridge Street
72 Broadway
73 Broadway

74

75

76

77

78

79

80

PREVIOUS PAGE

74 Lincoln Road
75 Barnack
76 Orton Hall
77 Cathedral Square
78 Cowgate
79 Westgate
80 Hampton Vale

THIS PAGE

81 Westgate
82 City Road
83 Exchange Street
84 Fletton
85 Westgate

82

85

Oriel windows pop up here and there to amuse and delight, projecting themselves by means of corbels, brackets or cantilevers from the main plane of a façade; in effect a bay, whether square, canted or, as in one instance here (**74**) triangular in plan, hoisted aloft. Barnack's propensity for architectural salvage furnishes this assemblage of Victorian Gothic incorporating older bits (**75**). Fully Victorian is the boldly corbelled example from Orton Hall (**76**).

Victorian too, but later, is the fancily bracketed oriel from Westgate (**81**), a building replete with surprising detail. More surprising detail accompanies the oriel (if it may be so described) which sits above the doorway in a re-entrant bay of a former pub in Cowgate (**78**). Versions of Classically derived orders and ornament adorning this very enjoyable late 19th-century confection defeat glib description. Here too is a modern attempt from Westgate (**79**), though the triangular oriel above the entrance to a school in Hampton (**80**) is perhaps more successful as a piece of design.

THIS PAGE

86 Priestgate
87 Queen Street
88 Burghley
89 Burghley Road
90 Woodston
91 Thorpe Hall
92 Thorney Abbey

NEXT PAGE

93 Alwalton
94 Minster Precincts: Infirmary
95 Newborough: St Bartholomew
96 Orton Waterville: St Mary
97 Alwalton: St Andrew
98 Orton Longueville: Holy Trinity
99 Sutton

It is difficult to be certain whether any of the blind windows shown here are strictly speaking a response to window tax. It is just possible that the examples from Priestgate (**86**) and Queen Street (**87**) are, though in both instances the infilled brickwork matches that of the surrounding walling both in brick type and bond. Perhaps more likely is that from Burghley (**88**), where some kind of detail at the head of the mullioned two-light window has been mutilated in the process. (Window tax was levied in various ways from the late 17th to the mid 19th century. Taxes on glass were removed in 1845, while window tax itself was repealed in 1851.)

More often than not blind windows, whether simulated or sealed, were simply a design solution to maintain the balance of a façade, a rhythm or pattern of fenestration or to relieve the blandness of an otherwise blank wall. In other cases internal layout and arrangements may have made a functioning window in a particular position impossible. Blank window apertures above shared passage entrances to Victorian terraces will usually be blind, since they often conceal the party wall line between houses. Burghley Road offers a typical arrangement, though sometimes a narrow window to light a small bedroom either side of the party wall could be squeezed in, as at Woodston (**90**), where a central mullion probably conceals the party wall.

Victorian examples of blind windows from the Thorpe Hall dairy (**91**) or from Edward Blore's Neo-Norman completion of a seemly east end for Thorney Abbey (**92**) are obviously design features, rather than some later blocking up. A feast of blocked window archaeology lies in the Minster Precincts Infirmary (**94**). Here a blocked 13th-century window has been provided, probably some time in the 15th century, with a new window lighting an inserted upper floor to the infirmary aisle. Blocked minor openings found on medieval churches may often be the result of some parsimonious repair or modification, or in some instances simply the filling up of a redundant image niche.

Arcading

Arcading is a series of arches supported upon columns or piers, as distinct from the column and beam, post and lintel arrangement of colonnades. Arcades may be 'open' as, say, in the nave arcades of most medieval churches, or 'blind' when attached to a wall to produce a rhythmical patterning.

The intermediate stage of Maxey's church tower (**1**) has, all around above a corbel table of masks and the like, a band of early 12th-century blind arcading flanking the two-light bell-openings. A similar mixture of blind and open arcading, though greatly enriched, wraps around the two main stages of Castor's church tower (**2**), probably the finest Norman crossing tower to a parish church in the country. The rich detail between the arcading suggests that the masons who erected this wondrous structure

THIS PAGE

1 Maxey: St Peter

THIS PAGE

2 Castor: St Kyneburgha
3 Minster Precincts: Great Gate
4 Sessions House, Thorpe Road
5 Thorney Abbey

were at least acquainted with what was going up between about 1120 and 1140 in the eastern parts of the Abbey church, now the Cathedral. Moreover its general appearance may provide clues as to the character of the long lost Romanesque Abbey's mid 12th-century crossing tower.

More Norman blind arcading (**3**) flanks a door opening within the Great Gate into the former monastic precinct from the Square. We are here in the later 12th century, by which time much of the blind arcading within the Abbey church itself was of the interlaced variety, the arches lapped right over left or left over right. Revived Norman style in the shape of the Victorian former Sessions House (**4**) deploys open arcading in two tiers above a gatehouse doorway.

15th-century figures occupying five ogee-headed niches high on the West Front of Thorney Abbey (**5**) form part of what, at a stretch, may be described as an arcade. They are high enough to have escaped the attentions of the casual iconoclast. Christ, second from left, wears a short robe to reveal his wounded feet. Second from right, holding a boat, is St Tatwin, a 7th-century anchorite who conveyed St Guthlac to his hermitage on the island of Croyland (now Crowland).

6

8

9

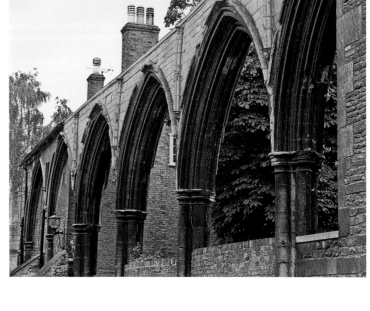

7

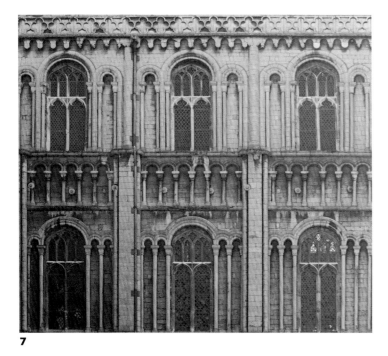

THIS PAGE

6 Cathedral
7 Cathedral
8 Minster Precincts: Infirmary
9 Minster Precincts: Infirmary

NEXT PAGE

10 Minster Precincts: Infirmary
11 Minster Precincts: Cloister
12 Minster Precincts: Cloister
13 Minster Precincts: Cloister

The Cathedral's external blind arcading has been variously adapted to accommodate enlarged windows; a process going on between the 13th and 15th centuries. This is evident in the Nave and South Transept, towards the cloister. Arcading to the Nave's intermediate storey was interrupted in the 14th century by the insertion of much larger segmentally headed windows with curvilinear tracery (**6**). The transept presents, in effect, a four-storey elevation, the upper three with tiers of arcading (**7**). The middle tier runs unbroken, whereas into those below and above has been inserted the Perpendicular tracery employed virtually throughout at clerestory level.

The arcading of the roofless ruins of the Abbey Infirmary (**8** and **9**) was originally entirely open. It remains so in part,

where post-Dissolution domestic adaptation of its aisles has also been lost. This mid 13th-century Infirmary was built on an astonishing scale. Patronage had come with royal connections and, with it, affinities to slightly earlier work at Winchester, as one or two surviving details on this and adjacent buildings testify. (The Infirmary's overall dimensions – a double cube – are very close to those of the Great Hall of Winchester Castle.) Finely moulded arches, capitals and an assortment of minor sculpture may still be readily enjoyed. Blind arcading beneath what would have been the West Window now shelters a reproduction Della Robbia Madonna and Child (**10**).

Much arcading survives in what remains of the cloister. Its southern wall (the monastic Refectory was on the other side)

retains complex patterns of blind arcading. To its eastern end Early English blank arcading with sub-arches is overlain with the remnants of later arcading (**11**). This relates to the vaulting systems of the cloister walks, all now lost. The western end of the same wall (**12**) retains, adjacent to the Refectory doorway, the rich Perpendicular panelling of a renewed Lavatorium (monks' wash-basins). The cloister west wall (once against the cellars) retains blank arcading above walling of considerable archaeological complexity (**13**). Amidst an assortment of blocked openings of various dates is material which may well be the earliest extant above-ground construction in central Peterborough.

16

Close inspection of the complex blind arcading of the Cathedral's West Front reveals some baffling details. On the one hand they offer some evidence for the abandonment of earlier designs for the back wall of the portico. (More fragmentary evidence of some of the many changes in the design made around 1200, as the work proceeded, is in the roof spaces above.) On the other hand the organisation of some of the interlaced blind arcading affords fertile ground for speculation as to the original intentions for the design as a whole.

Four details may illuminate this. A detail from the northernmost turret (**14**) has round-arched arcading appearing behind intersecting pointed arcading, yet all is in the same plane as if alluding to the Romanesque building beyond. Part of the back wall of the portico shows one layer of arcading seeming to disappear behind another (**15**), differently detailed and with an oddly irregular staccato rhythm, both layers again in the same plane. To add to the complexity a vaulting rib arrives, asymmetrically, in front of all this to be carried on a shaft which now makes little sense in terms of the overall design.

Image **16** shows slightly earlier mouldings, shaved off but for some reason suffered to remain, apparently grinning through in the same plane as the finished arrangement of arcading. Finally, at a lower level, a band of trefoil-headed blind arcading (**17**) wraps its way all round the portico. Its shafting alternates in colour; shafts of oolitic limestone alternating with shafts of Alwalton 'marble'. A hint perhaps that such variegation may have played a part in a dramatic polychromatic scheme of painted decoration, now almost entirely lost.

PREVIOUS PAGE

14 Cathedral: West Front
15 Cathedral: West Front
16 Cathedral: West Front

THIS PAGE

17 Cathedral: West Front

1

Door and Window Heads

Door and window heads offer a further design opportunity to express commercial, institutional or domestic status.

By focussing on the head of the superb Georgian doorway to Peterscourt (**1**) (seen also at page 16, number **11**) where its story is told) we can appreciate the meticulous detail of its full Corinthian entablature. Architrave, frieze and cornice are replete with all the elements correctly and precisely moulded and carved, while beneath is the distinctive Gothick fanlight with its daintily intersecting ogival and cusped miniature arches.

The main entrance to the former Trinity Presbyterian Church in Priestgate (**2**) is within a slightly projecting bay, its stonework heavily rusticated and the doorway itself boldly architraved with a so-called Gibbs surround (much deployed by James Gibbs:

THIS PAGE

1 Midgate

1662–1754). Within the arched head, beneath a huge console-bracketed keystone, is what can best be described as a blind fanlight – solid stone, but with equally boldly radiating 'lights'.

Banks and former banks, vying with one another for attention across Cathedral Square, adopt a variety of treatments; effectively engaging in a stylistic shouting match from their individually prominent positions. The hefty, vaguely Baroque treatment, at (**4**) contrasts with a much more restrained design opposite at the former Lloyds (**3**). In between, the old National Provincial, now NatWest (**5**), snootily asserts its earlier ancestry (Kirby Hall). A quaint stylistic contest in this digital age. Anyone for coffee?

A few yards along Bridge Street the Town Hall's main entrance maintains a dignified reticence in readiness for Armistice Day (**6**).

THIS PAGE

2 Priestgate
3 Cathedral Square
4 Cathedral Square/ Bridge Street
5 Cathedral Square
6 Bridge Street: Town Hall
7 Bridge Street

THIS PAGE

8 Cathedral: Cloister

NEXT PAGE

9 Peakirk
10 Glinton
11 Werrington
12 Cowgate
13 Eye

Architectural effusions at the door head are by no means an invention of the Renaissance and after. Witness the extraordinarily rich treatment given in the 13th century to the head of the doorway which greeted the monastic community entering their Refectory from the Cloister (**8**). Its lower, near round-headed opening carries exquisitely lush, deeply undercut stiff-leaf foliage. More of the same fills the spandrel between it and the fine mouldings (as complex as only 13th-century England could produce) of the main arch above, now surrounding a quatrefoil with attendant dragons in the undergrowth.

Fanlights at the door head come in a wide assortment of shapes and patterns, the term coming to be applied to any glazed opening above a door whether fan-shaped, or rectangular.

Semi-circular fanlights may adopt a number of decorative patterns. Simple radiating patterns are common (**9**) as are slightly more elaborate fan designs (**10**) or 'sunburst lights' (**11**, **12** and page 22, number **32**). Other fan-shaped forms include the 'batswing' (**13** and page 20, number **24**) and the similar 'teardrop' designs of the Regency.

Until the mid 18th century, radiating patterns or simple intersecting Gothick types (like that at page 22, number **31**), are likely to be made with glazing bars of wood. Thereafter, the more elaborate patterns in particular are often produced in metal – brass, wrought iron, moulded ribs of lead and compound versions with added ornament in cast lead.

14

17

15

16

18

PREVIOUS PAGE

14 Minster Precincts
15 Thorney
16 Priestgate
17 Deeping Gate
18 Eye

THIS PAGE

19 Priestgate
20 Broadway
21 Thorney
22 Westgate

At the hands of designers such as Robert Adam, the later 18th century was capable of producing fanlights of impressive decorative sophistication. Such advanced designs are scarce hereabouts, though a modest flavour of such elegance may be had from rectangular fanlights in Minster Precincts (**14**) and a Neo-Georgian example in Priestgate (**16**).

With the availability from the 1830s of polished sheet-glass, fancy fanlight design tended to decline. Plain fanlights of clear glass afforded an opportunity for little displays of *objets d'art*. At Deeping Gate (**17**) a row of jugs look especially fragile beneath the visual weight of a mighty rusticated lintel, fanlight incorporated.

Victorian speculative housing, whether in terraces or semi-detached 'villas', often incorporates a name at the door head, sometimes with a construction date. Nineteenth-century terraces may also carry a name and date on a plaque at a higher level, the name chiming with contemporaneous events, successful military campaigns overseas, etc. The origin of names at the door or window head may now be more difficult to place. Was Cromwell (**20**) the family name of the first owner, or was it expressing admiration for Oliver whose boys knocked Peterborough about a bit in 1643?

23

24

25

26

27

THIS PAGE

23 All Saints Road
24 All Saints Road
25 All Saints Road
26 Park Road
27 Fletton

In All Saints Road (in terraces dated 1905 carrying the initials SBB) both door heads and window heads for some reason carry the names of American States (**23**, **24** and **25**).

Victorian speculative builders' attempts to add a bit of ornament around the door or window head sometimes produce unintentionally comic touches which enliven the street scene. (such as the teetering orbs of **27**.)

More serious consideration was clearly given to the window heads of a retained façade in lower Bridge Street (**28**), elaborately executed in stone within pale gault brick pilastered walling. Equally

serious, and marking a high point of the bricklayers' art in the Edwardian period are two window heads from the former Carnegie Library in Broadway, one an oculus (**29**). Both have stone dressings in Edwardian Mannerist mode, set in finely executed red brickwork (Flemish bond) of the highest quality, that of (**30**) rubbed and gauged work with extremely fine joints run in lime putty. Facing Cathedral Square an upper series of windows (**31**), not content with a general Baroque swagger, are each endowed with a cartouche sitting on the keystone and in front of the cornice. (Pity about the netting.)

THIS PAGE

28 Bridge Street
29 Broadway
30 Broadway
31 Cathedral Square

29

31

32

34

33

35

36

38

39

PREVIOUS PAGE

32 Park Road
33 Manor House Street
34 Fletton
35 Orton Hall
36 Lincoln Road

THIS PAGE

37 Park Road
38 Park Road
39 Orton Waterville
40 Towler Street

40

More Edwardian Baroque swagger in Park Road (**32**), the window head larded with festoons of fruit and veg. An arched head to the former Catholic school in Manor House Street (**33**) carries, in its tympanum, a cartouche, its Cross Keys emblem of the Papacy behind the tiara doubly appropriate in Peterborough. A few years later the reticence of the Methodists on another similarly placed tympanum (**34**) stands in marked contrast.

More mundane domestic window heads allow themselves a little decoration here and there (**37**). In Towler Street (**40**) window and door heads are united under a common up and down label or hood mould, while a gable window from Orton Waterville has, equally unusually, a separate flat brick arch to each casement window light. (**39**).

On a grander note, returning to Orton Hall (**35**), we find the head of a bay window developed into a pierced parapet proclaiming its aristocratic pedigree with a mirrored depiction of the Gordon family (Marquesses of Huntly, Earls of Aboyne) monogram.

Window Tracery

Window tracery is the intersecting stone framework of mullions and transoms developed, at the window head, into geometric, curvilinear or rectilinear forms and patterns. The medieval development of the Gothic styles witnessed a general increase in the sizes of traceried windows, though as time went on, and partly from economic necessity, this was not necessarily accompanied by an increasing elaboration in tracery patterns.

This desire to increase the admission of light (seen as an embodiment of spirit) went hand-in-hand with advances in the techniques of stained glass production. Both played their part in the aesthetic developments associated with the theological thinking surrounding the medieval metaphysics of light, which assumed increasing architectural expression from the

PREVIOUS PAGE
1 Etton: St Stephen
2 Etton: St Stephen

THIS PAGE
3 Cathedral: South Transept
4 Northborough: St Andrew

12th century onwards. (The light of God 'was the stage lighting for the theatre of Gothic'). 'The astonishing idea of replacing opaque walls by transparent ones' facilitated the aesthetic notion of the 'wall veil'. Gothic architecture became increasingly diaphanous, its window tracery holding in place translucent panels 'vested' with sacred iconography.

The names given early in the 19th century to the styles of English Gothic – Early English, Decorated and Perpendicular – continue to have general currency. Very broadly speaking Early English was current for about a hundred years from the final quarter of the 12th century; the Decorated style from roughly the final quarter of the 13th century until the mid 14th century; and Perpendicular onwards for fully two centuries, well into the Tudor period.

The Perpendicular style was much the longest in duration; longer than the two preceding styles together, not least because the Renaissance – at least fully fledged architecturally – came late to these shores.

Attempting to date an entire structure from its window tracery alone requires caution. First there are overlapping transitional phases between the Gothic styles, just as there is between the Romanesque and the Gothic, often complicated by regional variations. Moreover a medieval wall can often be archaeologically complex in its own right, the window openings within it simply representing the last in a whole series of structural and stylistic changes.

5

6

Lancets – long narrow openings – characterise the earlier phase of the Early English style, used singly or in groups of two or three. At Etton, a remarkably complete 13th-century church, a group of five steeply climbing lancets produce a fine east window (**1**). A trio of lancets in revived Early English style light the tower space of St Paul's, New England, a church of 1868 paid for in large measure by the Great Northern Railway (**5**).

Plate-tracery represents the first development away from the lancet form, with the simple piercing of the flat surfaces at the head of a group. An original example may be seen to the louvred bell-openings in the tower at Alwalton (**7**), the flat surface pierced by simple quatrefoils, while a revived 19th-century example from Sutton (**8**) neatly illustrates the type.

7

Bar-tracery had been introduced initially at Westminster (courtesy of Rheims) before 1250. Its appearance accelerated the course of tracery development. Windows with quite complex geometrical patterns at the head soon became widespread. The Cathedral transepts retain several such windows (**9**), introduced perhaps in the 1270s or 1280s at the same time as construction of the now long lost Lady Chapel. Popular too at the end of the century was both so-called 'Y' tracery and, in larger windows, intersecting tracery. Stanground church which, chronologically speaking, roughly straddles 1300, affords good examples of both types, the former (**11**) lighting the chancel, the latter in the five-light east window (**10**), though here the cusping to the main lights may be due to restoration.

PREVIOUS PAGE

5   New England: St Paul
6   Northborough:
        St Andrew
7   Alwalton: St Andrew

THIS PAGE

8   Sutton: St Michael
9   Cathedral: South Transept
10 Stanground: St John the Baptist
11 Stanground: St John the Baptist

12

13

14

15

16

The ogee (double) curve made its Gothic reappearance some time in the 1290s facilitating, in all their forms the flowing curvilinear tracery patterns for which the Decorated style is famed. There is a sinuous suavity about the Decorated style as expressed in the first half of the 14th century; gone is the stiff crispness of much in the preceding style – a classic moment, 'a brilliant and sunny Spring' – whereas now, and particularly in the details, 'everything speaks of the blown petal'. Curvilinear tracery appears at higher levels in the Cathedral transepts (**12**), at Castor (**15**) and, quite spectacularly, at Northborough (**6**) where 14th-century patronage had attempted a lavish rebuilding on an extraordinary scale.

Roughly contemporary Reticulated (net-like) tracery graces

THIS PAGE

12 Cathedral: South Transept
13 Minster Precincts
14 Orton Longueville:
    Holy Trinity
15 Castor: St Kyneburgha
16 Northborough

NEXT PAGE

17 Barnack: St John
    the Baptist
18 Barnack: St John
    the Baptist

the east windows of Becket's Chapel, Minster Precincts (**13**), and Orton Longueville church (**14**), the latter with the ogees of its tracery lights elongated. Reticulations too, in a secular context, light the hall of Northborough Manor (**16**), a remarkable survival of hall and gatehouse. It will be noted that this hall window is straight-headed. Straight and shallow segmentally headed windows (an example of the latter from Barnack [**17**], beneath a band of characteristic ball-flower ornament) are not uncommon during the Decorated period. From Barnack too, but in a very different expression of the Decorated style, is the remarkable east window (**18**); a design – cusped and crocketed gables within each of five lancets – without any obviously directly comparable parallel, locally or nationally.

The essential elements of the Perpendicular (which in effect became the English national style, so enduring was it) were becoming apparent well before the mid 14th century. A tendency towards rectilinearity – a stiffening of reticulated forms, for example – had appeared in Norwich, London, Westminster and Gloucester in the 1320s and 1330s, with intimations elsewhere still earlier. So the Perpendicular was born well before the Black Death of 1348–9, though that cataclysmic event must have further concentrated minds in the direction of both aesthetic and economic rectitude.

Expression of the Perpendicular style in window tracery is typified by mullions which rush to the head of the arch without wavering or deflection. They meet or cut the horizontals at right angles, and frame rectilinear grids of panel tracery. Not that the ogee curve disappeared altogether, at least not immediately; rather it became subservient. The bell louvres to the tower of St John's church in the city centre (**19**) exhibit the form of unswerving mullion characteristic of the area (in the direction of Stamford and south Lincolnshire). The central mullion shoots straight up to the very apex of an arch which, though four-centred, seems almost rounded.

The Cathedral's New Building (**20** and **21**), famously fan-vaulted within, was constructed from around 1500 to envelop the apse which hitherto had risen sheer. This late

PREVIOUS PAGE

19 Cathedral Square: St John the Baptist
20 Cathedral: New Building

THIS PAGE

21 Cathedral: New Building
22 Marholm: St Mary

Perpendicular/Tudor design is usually attributed, on stylistic grounds alone, to the master mason John Wastell. (A contract does survive to prove Wastell's responsibility for completion of the fan vaults of King's College Chapel, Cambridge, vaults very similar in their details to those of the New Building.) Some have detected the same hand in the sophisticated Perpendicular of Marholm's chancel (**22**), quality work probably begun shortly after the New Building had been completed.

23

24

BOTH PAGES
23–27 Cathedral Square: St John the Baptist

Window tracery of the Victorian Gothic Revival refers back constantly to medieval precedent, but also accommodates all manner of personal interpretation and invention. If the Gothic Revival originated in the mid 18th century (though it can be argued that there was overlap between Gothic Survival and Revival a century before) it was to get into its stride in the wake of the brilliant polemic of Pugin and the Ecclesiologists in the 1830s and 1840s.

St John's in the city centre had commenced rebuilding on its present site at the beginning of the 15th century. A major restoration was undertaken in the 1880s by J L Pearson (at just about the same time as he was beginning to get into all manner of scrapes over his reconstruction of the Cathedral's crossing tower). The work included the provision of complete sets of large traceried windows to light the aisles north and south. Their tracery patterns are richly varied (**23** to **26**). They are, as has been said of a similarly varied set elsewhere, 'as appetising an assortment as a good box of chocolates'. Moreover they are convincing creations in an early Perpendicular style, as befits the building. Yet Pearson can have had no evidence for the prior existence of such; they must be flights of fancy of his own creative and scholarly imagination. Earlier 19th-century illustrations suggest that the whole church at that time was lit by windows exhibiting a uniform pattern of intersecting tracery; a few of these seem to remain towards the west end (**27**). But nor is this intersecting tracery likely to represent the original form as the type pre-dates the rebuilding by about a century (unless it had taken its cue from the earlier church sited east of the Cathedral).

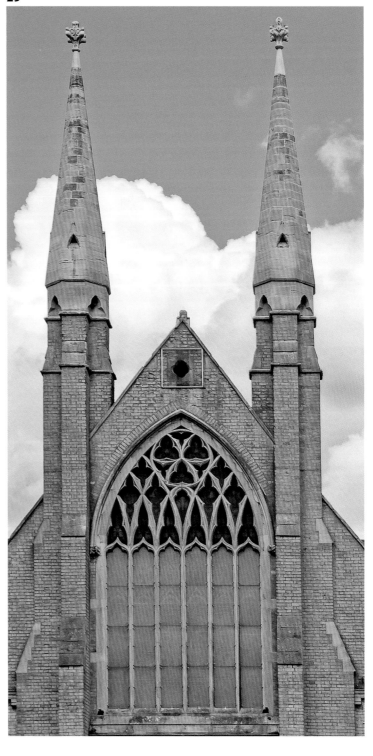

THIS PAGE

28 Park Road: All Souls
29 Westgate Church

NEXT PAGE

30 Geneva Street

Not long after Pearson's flights of fancy at St John's, the architect Leonard Stokes was providing designs for a new Catholic church in Geneva Street. A smaller version of his masterpiece, St Clare in Liverpool, All Souls (**28**) presents to Park Road a traceried East Window in a refined late Decorated/ early Perpendicular style (with Arts and Crafts leanings). It may well have been inspired by the late work of GF Bodley, with whom Stokes had worked and who, after Pearson's death in 1897, supervised completion of repairs to the Cathedral West Front whilst All Souls was abuilding.

Nonconformist churches were perfectly capable of adopting any one of a multiplicity of styles. When Revived Gothic was chosen it could be either fairly 'correct' in its details, as with Westgate Church (**29**) – the big six-light window an evocation of work around 1290, replete with trefoils in spherical triangles, ogees and much cusping, etc. (Obligingly, the Victorian stained glass – by Knowles of York – is backlit by night for the benefit of travellers exiting the bus station.) On the other hand, it could often be less than 'correct', producing wildly fanciful confections such as the amalgam of English Perpendicular and French Flamboyant (with Arts and Crafts touches) adorning the 1907 Baptist Church elevations both to Park Road and Geneva Street (**30**).

1

Chimneys and Roof Details

We risk missing out on all sorts of high-level fun and games due to our reluctance to raise our gaze. From chimneys crowning many a roof ridge, to eaves – the junction between roof and wall – we encounter a rich palette of materials and inventive forms.

First, two early survivals. Bold crockets climb the coping to the western gable of the 14th-century Hall of Northborough Manor to meet this exquisite and rare chimney-shaft at the apex (**2**). Hexagonal, and with tiny gables to each face (also with crockets as well as finials and pointed trefoils), this is a precious survivor from a time when such domestic sophistication was rare. Not far away in date, possibly a little earlier, is the splendid smoke louvre atop the Abbot's Gate in Minster Precincts, twin tiers of gabled trefoil-headed slots to each face (**6**).

THIS PAGE

1 Cathedral Square

2

3

4

5

6

Considering the wealth and quality of chimney stacks from the Tudor period surviving in East Anglia – bravura performances in brick and terracotta – it is surprising that our area has so few. Probably our best example – a cluster of four decorated brick chimneys at Paston Old Rectory – is now beyond public gaze due to recent development. A minor, later stack from the same building is pictured (**3**).

Some compensation for this gap is provided by the avalanche of 19th century chimneys taking their cue for high-spirited display, more or less, from Tudor exemplars. The Victorians, as always, were not averse to attempting to improve upon the prototypes; occasionally they succeeded, at least in terms of inventiveness. Some extraordinary confections, in stone rather than brick, may be enjoyed at Orton Hall (**4** and **5**) and Cathedral Square (**1**).

THIS PAGE

2   Northborough
3   Paston Ridings
4   Orton Hall
5   Orton Hall
6   Minster Precincts

7

8

9

10

11

THIS PAGE

7 Wansford
8 Wansford
9 Wansford
10 Priestgate
11 Lincoln Road

Brick examples usually make great play with caps corbelled out in stepped over-sailing courses, just as the prototypes. Patterns of Tudor derivation are sometimes reproduced on complete chimney-shafts of fired clay or, as at Paston, on tall pots atop stone or brick stacks. Decorative clay shafts and pots have often proved difficult and expensive to replicate if they have become dangerous due to their degree of exposure. They may have been replaced, as happened in Priestgate a decade or so ago (**10**) with simplified versions which, albeit of the right shape, are made of concrete.

THIS PAGE

12 Manor House Street
13 Burghley Road
14 Helpston
15 Orton Longueville
16 Midgate

In Lincoln Road (**11**) a cluster of brick stacks which might glibly be described as being in a 'Rogue-Goth's' version of Tudor. At Wansford, an assortment of brick stacks surmount stone flue shafts to a house replete with much 'Rogueish' detail. No surprise here, since this was in all probability designed by SS Teulon, the 'Rogue-Goth' architect familiar from Thorney where he also designed much for the Duke of Bedford. As at Thorney, so at Wansford, though much of what is likely to be Teulon's work is across the river in Huntingdonshire, and so beyond our scope.

This particular building in Old North Road (**7**) is Peterborough territory and executed in Teulon's very personal take on Tudor. Built specifically for the Duke's cooper it carries, in addition to the Duke's coat of arms and a barrel bearing the cooper's monogram on the front elevation (**8**), a 'B' for Bedford on the stone chimney breast (**9**). The organisation of this chimney breast and its twin brick stacks on the gable-end wall demonstrates some of the care and originality which Teulon brought to his distinctive, idiosyncratic detailing.

16

PETERBOROUGH and its villages IN DETAIL

17

18

19

20

21

22

23

THIS PAGE

17 Thorpe Hall
18 Glinton
19 Orton Longueville
20 Etton
21 Thornhaugh
22 Orton Longueville
23 Northborough

NEXT PAGE

24 Pilsgate

Particularly to the west of the city centre, chimney stacks surviving from the 17th and 18th centuries, whether 'polite' (e.g. Thorpe Hall) or 'vernacular' (e.g. Glinton), are often of stone. Thorpe Hall's roofscape proudly carries four mighty stone chimney shafts describing its flat top, four-square like the house itself (**17**). Each has rusticated masonry and is capped with an elaborate cornice. Within these stacks originally rose a central belvedere lantern (fashionable in the second half of the 17th century, from which to enjoy the prospect) accessed from within by a great spiral stair which happily survives. (Such belvederes are now comparatively rare; several have been lost to fires. Sad to record therefore that, just as this is being written, fire has destroyed the late 17th-century Cupola House

in Bury St Edmunds where a fine survivor crowned the roof.)

At a vernacular level stone stacks, and occasionally brick ones, are sometimes split to form twin flue shafts separated by a small gap. Sometimes trios of slightly separated stone flues may be found. At Orton Longueville the middle flue-shaft rather surprisingly carries a sundial (**19**). The splendid divided stack from Glinton has rusticated masonry to the twin shafts, which together carry a chunk of full entablature (**18**). (A recent study comparing vernacular stone architectural details of the Cotswolds and what it termed the Stamford Region – both having ready access to comparable Jurassic limestones – noted that, despite many similarities, divided examples appeared to be confined largely to the north and west borders of our area.)

No apology is necessary for revisiting Burghley's singular skyline here; this is surely the most memorably distinctive of the Elizabethan/Jacobean age in the country. The chimney shafts, famously comprising Tuscan columns clustered in groups of two, three and four, are an astonishing conceit (**25** and **26**). All carry great chunks of entablature and, not content with that, 'pots', (if so prosaic a term may be applied), resembling miniature castellated towers. However, not all of Burghley's chimneys are so grand. Ancillary buildings carry more mundane practical solutions to smoke dispersal which nevertheless sport some nice clay pots with Neoclassical inflections (**27** and **28**).

PREVIOUS PAGE

25 Burghley

THIS PAGE

26 Burghley
27 Burghley
28 Burghley

31

When it comes to the inner urban area, the chimneyscape, so to speak, is largely a story of competing variants on simplified Tudor themes. Either that or long phalanxes of stacks bestriding the ridges of 19th-century terraces, bristling with TV aerials and often a bewildering variety of clay pots, some disconcertingly tottery. Here and there we find some more interesting recent efforts and a sprinkling of oddities, such as that in Cowgate (**33**). (Can this really have been a functioning stack?) A shiny cluster of flues, quite sculpturally grouped and coordinated, has recently appeared to adorn the skyline at the City Hospital, looming above Soke Parkway (**29**).

THIS PAGE

29 City Hospital
30 Priestgate
31 Fletton

THIS PAGE
32 New England
33 Cowgate
34 Fletton
35 Broadway

36

37

38

THIS PAGE

36 Etton
37 Minster Precincts
38 Priestgate

NEXT PAGE

39 Bridge Street
40 Etton
41 Bishops Road

Scanning down the roof from the ridge we encounter a very varied range of materials covering the slopes: plain clay tiles, pantiles, an assortment of interlocking tiles, Welsh slate, Collyweston stone slate (a fissile limestone) and, spread more widely over the whole area than might be expected, considerable quantities of thatch. Straddling as it does the Fen edge, the area often throws up surprising conjunctions of materials, as at Etton where, at a junction of roof slopes, walls and chimney stack, stone, stock brick, pantile and thatch all coexist comfortably (**36**).

It is worth looking in detail at the way in which Collyweston slate roof cladding is handled where the main slope is required to return through ninety degrees to meet that of a dormer, wing or projecting bay. The valley so formed cannot easily be drained by means of a lead valley gutter, as might be the case with say plain clay tiling, and is therefore 'swept' around (as they would say in the Cotswolds) without a sharp angle, by means of a 'lacing' together of stone slates. This 'turning' of the valley, as it is more usually termed in these parts, is a highly skilled operation. Examples illustrated are from Minster Precincts (**37**) and Priestgate (**38**).

43

44

45

Popping out from many a roof slope, and organised either formally or in random fashion, dormer windows lighting roof storeys add to the variety and interest.

Considerable care and attention has been paid both to the design and detailing of the row of dormers nestling behind the parapet of the early Georgian terrace in Minster Precincts (**42**), set within a Collyweston roof laid, as is customary, in courses diminishing towards the ridge. Each dormer has its own pitched roof with little turned valleys, a plain clay tiled ridge and is fronted with a pediment. The cheeks are weatherboarded. The little pediments are either triangular (a) or segmental (b) (**43**)

and because of their even number are grouped: a – b – b – a, rather than: a – b – a – b – a, as would be expected with an uneven number. Focussing down closer to a dormer with segmental pediment (echoing in miniature those to the doorcases below) above a full cornice (which even has vestigial triglyphs underneath) it is possible to detect that the side-hung casement retains its wrought iron strap hinges (**43**).

Dormers appear in all shapes, sizes and styles. Even churches occasionally sport the odd dormer. Improvements to the clerestory lighting of the mid 19th-century St Mark's, Lincoln Road necessitated the introduction, in 1906, of a

48

large three-light gabled half-timbered dormer within the roof slope (**47**). Eyebrow dormers, like that at Alwalton (**44**), were a speculative house-builders' favourite both before and after World War II. Another detail from the former almshouses in Westgate shows a gabled dormer (**48**) with fancy bargeboards wedged, visually, between two tall chimney stacks, confirming the picturesque Tudorising makeover to which the building was subjected in 1837. Twin storeys within a Collyweston roof (**46**) show how carefully the stone slating needs to be organised around nicely staggered dormers in close proximity to the precisely formed hipped end.

PREVIOUS PAGE

42 Minster Precincts
43 Minster Precincts
44 Alwalton
45 Longthorpe

THIS PAGE

46 Sacrewell
47 Lincoln Road: St Mark
48 Westgate

51

Some nice juxtapositioning of materials – in thatch, render, timber, stone, brick (in Flemish bond), pantile and Collywestons – will be appreciated with the example from Orton Longueville (**49**). The thatch, in combed reed fairly recently renewed, looks particularly trim and tidy, almost sculptural or moulded in its careful formation around gables and at the ridge copings. These latter will often be executed in more malleable material, say in sedge, providing great scope for the thatcher to display individualistic scallop or zigzag patterning. Herein lies one of the most attractive aspects of the material which has made it especially suitable for the *cottage orné* style, an aspect of the cult of the Picturesque.

For many centuries in much of England the standard material used for thatching was long straw. As a material long straw produced the rather more shaggy appearance to the roofs of cottages and the like, familiar from many an old print, rather than the neat and tidily trimmed verges, gables, dormers, etc., possible with combed reed. Sometimes much older straw thatch survives beneath a more recent thatch of combed reed. A great thickness of thatch evident at, say, a gable-end wall, may be an indicator. (The example from Orton Waterville (**57**) may be just such an instance). Occasionally the straw beneath may be found to be smoke blackened and so of considerable age and archaeological value.

PREVIOUS PAGE

49 Orton Longueville
50 Orton Longueville
51 Northborough

THIS PAGE

52 Alwalton
53 Orton Waterville
54 Orton Waterville
55 Upton
56 Orton Waterville
57 Orton Waterville

THIS PAGE

58 Maxey
59 Maxey
60 Longthorpe

NEXT PAGE

61 Barnack
62 Orton Waterville
63 Maxey
64 Orton Waterville
65 Ailsworth
66 Maxey
67 Late of Marholm

It is a fairly common sight to see an assortment of farmyard and domestic animals, birds, etc., sculpted in straw and cavorting about upon the ridges of thatched roofs. This appears to be a comparatively modern development of the thatcher's art, belonging perhaps to the realm of folk art rather than strictly to the vernacular tradition. Nonetheless, it represents a hugely entertaining departure and is greatly appreciated, even if somewhat high maintenance – one or two examples have come to look a little threadbare.

61

62

63

64

65

66

67

The junction between roof slope and wall at the eaves offers great scope for decorative invention, whether by means of parapet design or some form of eaves cornice. Parapets may be simple and unadorned, say of brick with a plain stone coping sloped to run the water off to a gutter behind. On the other hand stone parapets can offer greater opportunities for display. They may be kitted out with Classical mouldings, crenellated (battlemented), elaborately pierced with openwork (**69**) or provided with lengths of open balustrading through which dormers may peep.

PREVIOUS PAGE

68 Church Street

THIS PAGE

69 Orton Hall
70 Priestgate
71 Lincoln Road
72 Priestgate

Projecting eaves may be formed in a number of ways. Very deeply projecting eaves carrying a gutter to their outer edge will require substantial brackets to support a broad soffit board (on the underside). These afford great scope for decoration in themselves. Eaves cornices tend, on the whole, to adopt some sort of derivative of the Classical cornice. Notional or actual support may be provided either by variations on the shaped bracket, repeated singly or arranged in pairs, or by mouldings of Classical derivation (mutules, modillions, rows of dentils as at

the Great Northern Hotel [**75**], etc.). In Lincoln Road projecting eaves are enlivened by a touch of Oriental uplift at the hip (**77**).

The Victorians, ever inventive, managed to come up with an assortment of variants whose antecedents are less easy to place. A case in point is from Fletton (**74**) where paired brackets carry, at their ends, little drops resembling bobbins. Awkward conjunctions between differing roof slopes (**78**), or between roof and walls adjoining neighbouring buildings (**81**), often called for considerable ingenuity in handling the eaves detail.

PREVIOUS PAGE
73 Dogsthorpe
74 Fletton
75 Station Road
76 Thorpe Hall Dairy

THIS PAGE
77 Lincoln Road
78 Lincoln Road
79 Wothorpe
80 Westgate
81 Broadway

Rainwater Heads, Gutters and Downpipes

Precipitation being what it is in Britain, efficient means of rainwater disposal has always been a consideration. However, necessity being the mother of invention, opportunities have often been taken to elevate the fittings required to the status of another design opportunity with the addition of ornament, dates, coats of arms or even the conversion of the system into a water feature (**2**).

The rainwater head or hopper head, a small cistern or tank at the head of the downspout, will be the most usual recipient of any decorative flourish, whether integral or applied. The splendid cast lead example (**1**) from the Cathedral's New Building seems more than an expression of some sort of bastion – perhaps an evocation of a whole celestial city.

THIS PAGE

1   Cathedral: New Building

4   5   6   7

Many a gutter has been glimpsed already, above eaves cornices and the like. Some eaves may originally have lacked any form of guttering at all. These will probably now be found with a system of guttering laid to falls by means of adjustable metal brackets (**3**). Concealing gutters behind parapets has long been common practice in more formal buildings. The associated downpipes may then also be hidden in the building structure, be external (**5**), or dispensed with altogether (**6**). Overflow spouts (**4**) are increasingly needed to cope with heavier downpours.

THIS PAGE

2 Rivergate:
   Crown Courts Building
3 Bishops Road/Minster
   Precincts
4 Alwalton: St Andrew
5 Great Northern Hotel
6 Longthorpe
7 Burghley Road

8

9

10

11

12

13

14

15

PREVIOUS PAGE

8 Minster Precincts
9 Thorney
10 Cathedral Square
11 Westgate
12 Ufford
13 Orton Hall
14 Welland Road
15 Aldermans Drive

THIS PAGE

16 Ufford
17 Ufford
18 Cathedral Square:
    St John the Baptist
19 Cathedral Square
20 Cross Street

Dated rainwater hoppers are quite common, in both cast lead and cast iron. In Minster Precincts (**8**) an ambitious hopper, dated 1728, indicates the construction date of the terrace. It also carries the Fitzwilliam arms above some ebullient Classical egg-and-dart and anthemion ornamentation, all cast lead. Many of the hoppers from St John's Church in the city centre carry the date 1819 (**18**), the date of the first of two comprehensive restorations in the 19th century. It was the impact of the 1819 restoration which Pearson, in the 1880s, did his best to sweep away as decidedly 'incorrect'.

19   20

Brick, Stone and Terracotta

Originally, brick-making locally was a small-scale seasonal activity; a craft industry employing seasonal labour, responding to fluctuating local demand and requiring little capital outlay. A more substantial brickyard, complete with kiln for lime burning and a coke oven as well as a brick kiln, is recorded in the late 18th century as having operated in Stanground. Some villages around Peterborough retained their own clay pits until late into the 19th century; Thorney's for instance, solely serving the estate upon which it lay. From the 1870s onwards the Fletton brick industry became synonymous with the large-scale mass-production of common (as distinct from facing) bricks, exploiting the Lower Oxford clays – 'the clay that burns'.

THIS PAGE

1 Midgate

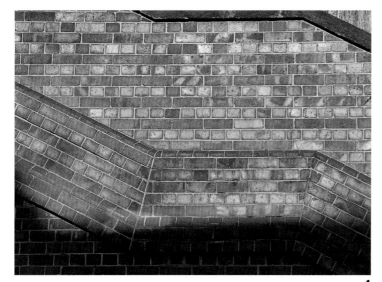

A typical story is that of Eye's industry. In 1835 a pit was opened to produce bricks for new farm buildings. Close by, at Eye Green, in the 1890's a substantial parcel of land rich in high quality clays, gravels and sands was acquired. Thus the Northam Brick Company (later to be absorbed by the London Brick Company) came into being, wide distribution of its products greatly facilitated by the construction of a rail link. An aerial ropeway between Eye and new sources of clay at Dogsthorpe Pit was constructed in 1928. Following closure, the workings at Eye Green became filled with water from natural springs and now form a nature reserve (**2**).

With the arrival of the railways it became possible to import bricks from further afield for Peterborough's buildings, as well as exporting them, and brick became ubiquitous. The local character of the brick-built parts of central Peterborough was transformed by mass-produced products from near and far complementing the output of the local companies such as the Peterborough Patent Brick and Tile Company.

THIS PAGE

2   Eye
3   Orton Longueville
4   River Lane/Crescent Bridge
5   Bourges Boulevard
6   Broadway

11

THIS PAGE

7 Orton Longueville

8 Broadway

9 Bridge Street

10 Orton Waterville

11 Newborough

The character of a traditionally constructed building is affected to a great extent by the patterns and textures of its areas of solid walling. In brickwork the pattern will be dependent upon the brick bond used; that is, the arrangement of 'headers' and 'stretchers' in each brick course and the way strength is imparted by avoiding continuous vertical joints.

With the departure of the Romans, brick-making in Britain seems to have been all but forgotten for the best part of a millennium. Its first serious revival, in the 14th century, witnessed a rather random and homespun approach to bonding. The first regular pattern to become established was English bond – alternating courses of all headers and all stretchers (**7**). English bond remained paramount through the Tudor period.

12

13

14

15

16

THIS PAGE

12 Minster Precincts
13 Minster Precincts
14 Wheel Yard
15 North Street
16 Gladstone Street

More recent examples are **4** (page 127), **8** and **9**. In the latter case the English bond, in a nice handmade facing brick, is 'broken' by additional headers in the stretcher course and by a vent formed with a tile creasing.

From the first half of the 17th century English bond gradually gave way to Flemish, comprising alternate headers and stretchers in the same course (**10**) (this nice brickwork spoiled by modern weatherstruck pointing). In **11** the original flush pointing survives. Regarded as more ornamental, and to a degree more economical (if slightly less strong too), Flemish bond has generally been the favoured bond subsequently, though both continued to be used in parallel until the necessity for the monotonously dull stretcher bond was imposed by the advent of cavity walling.

There are many other arrangements by which bricks may be bonded. In Minster Precincts, for instance (**12** and **13**), is an example of irregular bond, probably 18th century, without any consistent pattern. A modern curved wall at the entrance to the Wheel Yard (**14**) is in English garden-wall bond – three courses of stretchers to one of headers. Header bond, that is headers only to every course, is rarely used for a whole building, though it may be spotted in the shallow curved Regency bays of seaside towns. It is most useful for tightly curving brickwork such as the recessed North Street corner of the Ostrich Inn (**15**) and the Gladstone Street mosque (**16**).

17

18

19

20

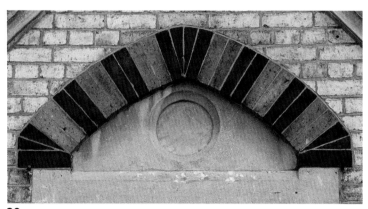

THIS PAGE

17 Lincoln Road
18 Lincoln Road
19 Park Road
20 Park Road

NEXT PAGE

21 Alwalton
22 Midgate
23 Park Road

Ornamental brickwork, from diaper patterning as in Midgate (**1**, page 126) to that which is moulded or even carved (**17**) and (**18**), is represented in Peterborough by 19th-century revivals of techniques developed from the 15th through to the 18th century. Tudor diapers were usually made with headers, bricks with the most heavily burnt, often vitrified, ends being chosen. The Victorians, ever resourceful, were adept at playing similar games, but with all the gusto that a wider palette of coloured machine-made bricks allowed (**19**, **20** and **21**). Tumbled brickwork to gables or chimney breasts (**22**) and the like could also receive the polychromatic treatment (**23**).

The 20th century did not give up entirely on the notion of ornamental brickwork. The pronounced vertical emphasis of the decorative brick forms to the entrance façade of Woodston Baptist Church (**27**) imparts something of the flavour of continental Expressionism. In North Street, what might otherwise be a very dull blank wall in stretcher bond to the flank of Westgate House (**28**) is greatly redeemed by the use of slightly contrasting bricks defining blind panels which project and recede. A gable end wall (**29**) is imaginatively enlivened with a design in contrasting brickwork, though just what the symbolism (if any) might be is unclear.

THIS PAGE

24 Lincoln Road
25 Boroughbury (Lincoln Road)
26 Peakirk

NEXT PAGE

27 Oundle Road
28 North Street
29 Gladstone Street
30 Cowgate

27

28

29

30

31

32   **33**

34

THIS PAGE

31 Barnack: St John the Baptist
32 Marholm: St Mary
33 Thorpe Hall
34 Westgate

NEXT PAGE

35 Wittering: All Saints
36 Wittering: All Saints
37 Church Street: St John the Baptist
38 Church Street: St John the Baptist

The character of stonework elevations can be determined largely by the manner in which the masonry is arranged in courses, or not, and whether the individual stones are squared, dressed, rough-dressed, quarry-faced or rubble. The pre-Conquest origin of the churches at Barnack and Wittering is evident from their distinctive stonework. The roughly dressed and coursed masonry of the upper stage of Barnack's tower (**31**) is divided into panels by a series of long thin pilaster-like strips – lesenes – with the quoins formed in equally characteristic 'long-and-short-work'.

Long-and-short-work at Wittering (**35** and **36**) defines very clearly the original form and proportion of both Chancel and Nave in this substantial Saxon survival.

Fine 16th-century ashlar masonry – accurately cut, dressed, squared and laid with the finest jointing – may be seen to the south side of Marholm's chancel (**32**). (The south side is very much the show front, towards the approach from the great house, Milton; the Chancel's north side is much less expensively clad.) Examples of 17th- and 18th-century ashlar are from Thorpe Hall (**33**) and Westgate (**34**). In both these cases

the buff and pink tinges suggest that the freestone used is Ketton. Probably the finest example of 18th-century ashlar masonry is that on the Palladian south front of Milton (architect, Henry Flitcroft) but this is beyond our gaze here. From St John's Church we can see that other masonry treatments produce quite different patterns and textures. Buttresses at its west end are finished in roughly dressed stone supporting otherwise uncoursed random rubble (**37**). By contrast, the staircase to the room over the porch (**38**) is finished with large stones, squared but not regularly coursed.

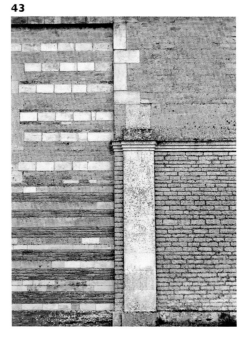

41

42

44

Banded masonry in various forms – such as alternating courses of squared and random rubble or of ashlar and quarry-faced stones – is found throughout the area, from the early 16th century in Minster Precincts (**39**) through to the 18th (**40** and **41**) and mid 19th centuries (**42**). A quite instructive illustration of how different masonry patterns affect texture may be seen with the close juxtaposition of several to one of the Burghley lodges (**43**).

Patterns and textures of walling may be interrupted by an assortment of interventions, intended or otherwise. At Castor (**44**) a coursed rubble wall is suddenly interrupted by a large outcrop of herringbone masonry, clearly ancient. This we must now learn to recognise as a fragment of the Roman

Praetorium, rather than a villa as had been assumed. The stone coursing to the external face of Thorpe Hall's great encompassing garden wall is punctuated at intervals all round by paired niches (in which to converse whilst enjoying the prospect) (**45**). Stone barns, often now converted to domestic use, will usually have the additional patterning of former air circulation vents. These may simply be small triangular apertures at regular intervals (**46**), though at Ufford the coursed 18th-century stonework is graced by several fine large ventilation lunettes with keyblocks and diaper pattern infill (**47**).

A couple of surviving examples are illustrated of a pattern of walling which, to judge from old photographs, was once more common in Peterborough than now. In both what appears to

be rusticated stonework, painted, is more likely to be stucco in one of its forms, heavily rusticated to resemble ashlar-work. At (**48**) the rustication is V-jointed, and at (**49**) channel-jointed, both types familiar from masonry.

PREVIOUS PAGE

39 Minster Precincts
40 Longthorpe
41 Glinton
42 Orton Hall
43 Barnack Road
44 Castor

THIS PAGE

45 Thorpe Hall
46 Castor
47 Ufford
48 Exchange Street/ Cathedral Square
49 Exchange Street/Cumbergate

50

51

52

53

54

THIS PAGE

50 Broadway
51 Park Road
52 Woodston
53 Gladstone
54 Orton Waterville
55 Aldermans Drive

NEXT PAGE

56 Gladstone
57 Park Road
58 Woodston
59 Helpston
60 Helpston

55

Terracotta ('baked or cooked earth') varies in colour when unglazed, according to that of its constituent clay. It is closely related to brick, but with its decoration generally received from plaster moulds. Before the 19th century the use of terracotta in England would have been solely for ornamental purposes. Subsequently, some architects have been accused of overloading buildings with it. Sometimes entire buildings were clad (e.g. Alfred Waterhouse's Natural History Museum, South Kensington).

But for the average speculative builder this mass-produced product came in very handy as a relatively inexpensive way of adding a bit of Classical ornament – say a bit of egg and dart (**50**), a decorative frieze (**51** and **52**), roundels or patterning

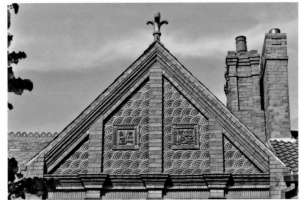

59

60

in the gable (**56** and **57**) or an individual patera to fill the odd space (**54**). Often such terracotta decoration is used in combination with brick 'specials' formed to specific shapes, and it can sometimes be difficult to distinguish between the two. A roofline might be given a Gothic touch with a mythical beast or two in terracotta (courtesy of Viollet-le-Duc?), applied to the ridge (**55**).

By the latter half of the 19th century terracotta products, like brick of all descriptions, were ubiquitous. It may be difficult to pin down a specific manufacturer unless a maker's stamp is spotted. The nearest of the Midlands manufactures to Peterborough was in Stamford. JM Blashfield, a sculptor who had worked in the Coades' factory, purchased various

moulds and models when that firm closed down in the 1830s. In 1858 he moved his operation from Poplar to Stamford where it continued until 1875 (though soon without Blashfield himself). It may be that Terra Cotta [sic] House at Wothorpe (page 21, number **30**) is built with Blashfield's terracotta, though the date over the doorway is a little after the firm's closure.

An endearing use of terracotta is on the 1919 Victory Cottage at Helpston, a house in which all the materials in this section of the book are featured (**59** and **60**). There is a generous use of terracotta in friezes, keyblocks, cornices, etc., and victory in WW1 is celebrated with a liberal sprinkling of brightly coloured broken tile, applied kaleidoscope fashion. (Perhaps Helpston's answer to Gaudi's tile encrusted Parque Güell, Barcelona!)

1

Clockfaces and Sundials

The clock on the Bridge Street façade of the Town Hall (**1**) was originally commissioned in 1868 to grace a jeweller's shop close to its present position in Narrow Bridge Street (though on a building line well to the west) from where, probably for the first time in Peterborough, it proudly announced 'Railway Time'. Following the demolition of Narrow Bridge Street it adorned the old Carnegie Library in Broadway, where the remote skeleton mechanism could be seen behind glass just inside the entrance. Upon sale of that building the clock was put into storage, but in 2005 brought out, repaired and commendably installed at the Town Hall by the City Council.

Roman numerals predominate, even on modern commercial examples (Darcy's [**2**] is an exception), though the Guildhall clock (**3**) obligingly offers Arabic numerals for the minutes, at the quarters.

THIS PAGE

1 Bridge Street: Town Hall

2

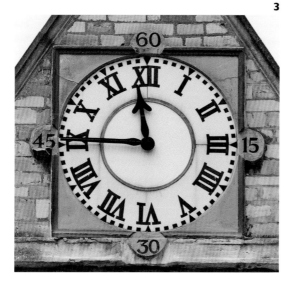

3

4

5

6

7

At Barnack (**4**) the elegant Roman numerals find themselves squeezed between the relative crudities of Saxon interlace, lesenes and foliate carving.

Clocks were occasionally commissioned to commemorate specific events. The large bracket clock projecting above Park Road (**5**) was installed in 1921 and dedicated by the then Bishop of Peterborough before a large gathering as a memorial to thirty-one employees of the Peterborough Equitable Industrial Co-operative Society who perished in WW1. Difficulties may arise with clocks carrying brand names (**6**) or those of family businesses (**2**) should they relinquish their premises. Public clocks presenting several faces to the world (**7**) inspire confidence only if they give precisely the same time information in each direction!

THIS PAGE

2 Westgate
3 Cathedral Square: Guildhall
4 Barnack: St John the Baptist
5 Park Road
6 Bridge Street
7 Alwalton
8 Cathedral Square/ Bridge Street

8

10

The earliest surviving sundials are probably Saxon mass or 'tide' dials and the scratch dials often found on the sides of later medieval churches, particularly on or around the south porch. (Though rebuilding or enlargement of a porch may have obliterated or damaged an earlier dial or led to relocation on other walls.) The Saxon daylight hours were divided into four 'tides', each of three hours. The dial was therefore divided into four divisions below a horizontal line upon which was fixed the *gnomon* – set at noon on Midsummer's Day. Sometimes intermediate divisions are introduced, producing seven radii in all, cut by short lines at right angles to indicate the times at which masses were to be celebrated. The circular dial on Barnack church tower (**9**) may have been just such an example. The divisions below the diameter have been eroded away, though the hole for the *gnomon* remains clear.

The later and much more numerous scratch dials (not to be confused with Ordnance Survey bench marks (**10**) often found on church towers) fulfilled the same primary function: to ensure that the bell was rung correctly for the canonical hours. They are sometimes circular and inscribed with the twelve divisions of the day, though the example here (**11**) maintains the seven radii below the *gnomon* of many Saxon predecessors.

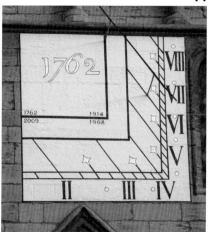

Much the strangest and rarest sundial in the area is that standing in a field by Upton Church (**12**). One of a species of 'lectern sundials' designed for specific astronomical investigation (and possibly associated with Freemasonry), most surviving examples seem to be in Scotland. This one was measured and drawn by the antiquary John Carter, who believed it to have been made in the reign of Charles I. His drawings, which render the object a good deal more intelligible than a photograph is able, were published in 1819. (Copies are usually held in the church.)

PREVIOUS PAGE

9 Barnack:
   St John the Baptist
10 Stanground:
   St John the Baptist
11 Orton Waterville

THIS PAGE

12 Upton
13 Priestgate
   (i.e. in yard off)
14 Cathedral: West Front
15 Cathedral:
   New Building
16 Marholm

17

18

19

20

THIS PAGE

17 Helpston
18 Burghley Road
19 Castor: St Kyneburgha
20 Cathedral Square: Guildhall

NEXT PAGE

21 Paston: All Saints
22 Helpston

Mottoes and dedications, whether on clocks or sundials, tend mainly to be in Latin; *Tempus Fugit* (**8**) or, occasionally, *Hora Fugit* (**17**), being the most common. Whilst these unhelpfully remind us that time flies, *Resurgam* (essentially 'I shall rise again') is nicely ambiguous (**20**); both a reference to the sun, and a shout of triumph by the Royalist sponsors of the Guildhall at the Restoration of the monarchy in 1660. The same legend appears prominently – a Phoenix rising from the flames – on Wren's St Paul's Cathedral, rebuilt after the Great Fire of 1666.

From quite an early date the positioning of many a sundial hardly seems conducive to legibility. That mounted on a triple-flued stone stack from Orton Longueville (page 104, number **19**)

carries a mid 17th-century date. At Castor a sundial appears visually to balance precariously above an acutely pointed transept window (**19**). Since 1756 Paston's chancel gable seems to have carried a sundial mounted rather improbably on a sort of crude cartouche, in the position where one might more usually see a foliated cross (**21**).

Some of the sundials illustrated here have been set up much more recently than may be expected. A plaque close to the sundial (**22**) (which even marks the half-hours) tells us it was set up in 1933. A simpler version, bearing the owner's initials, dates from 1964 (**17**).

Carvings

The working and shaping of hard materials – stone, wood, even brick – is an age-old tradition. Carving, *per se*, better describes those parts of buildings which, having been worked into planes, shapes, mouldings, etc., are afforded particular emphasis or significance by the addition of decoration. This may be as repeated ornament, say between shafting or in a frieze, or may be concentrated upon more sculpted forms, say a capital, a figure in a niche or a series of grotesques.

Close proximity to the many quarries of the Jurassic limestone belt (the Inferior Oolites of the Lincolnshire limestone formations) has yielded a range of building stones, from the famed Barnack ragstone with which the Cathedral is largely but by no means exclusively constructed, to a range of freestones more amenable

to finely finished and carved work. Several of these quarries had been worked by Romans and Saxons; techniques for extraction, manipulation and working were thus developed early.

The Cathedral and its precincts are replete with carved work and sculpture from the Saxon period through the Romanesque (or Anglo-Norman) and into the Gothic era. Much from the 13th century remains to the Cathedral's exterior, particularly around the portico of the West Front. Capitals of lush stiff-leaf are readily visible (**1** and **2**), their ruffled stylised leaves of the 'windblown' variety. Towards the Cloister a roughly contemporary doorway (**3**) sports long runs of boldly undercut dog-tooth ornament between the shafting. Above a doorway opposite, a search amongst the foliage reveals a dragon (**4**) (see also page 80, number **8**).

PREVIOUS PAGE

1   Cathedral

THIS PAGE

2   Cathedral
3   Cathedral
4   Cathedral: Cloister

5

6

7

THIS PAGE

5 Minster Precincts

6 Minster Precincts

7 Minster Precincts

NEXT PAGE

8 Church Street: St John the Baptist.

9 Minster Precincts

10 Minster Precincts

The Prior's Gate in Minster Precincts, (seen in its entirety on page 26, number **47**), carries a collection of carved emblems, including the rebus of Abbot Robert Kirkton who was responsible for its construction. Its main frieze, above the archway, has, amidst assorted Tudor emblems (**5**) and heraldry (including the arms of St Edward the Confessor [**6**]), Westminster being a powerful related Benedictine house), a Trinitarian emblematic device – the *Scutum Fidei* or Shield of Faith (**7**). Its Latin inscriptions may no longer be decipherable, but this device had become very popular by the end of the Middle Ages. What makes its presence here interesting is that it was almost certainly an invention of Robert Grosseteste, proto-scientist and sometime reforming Bishop of Lincoln (in whose vast diocese Peterborough then lay), who in 1238 dedicated the Abbey Church but a few feet away.

The stone vaulting within the open porch of St John's is readily visible. The principal boss (the carved 'keystone' at the junction of vaulting ribs) conveys another representation of the Trinity (**8**). (Yet another is to be found on a boss in a similar position within the Cathedral porch.) The St John's example is of a type known to art historians as a *Gnadenstuhl* (Seat of Grace) Trinity. This form tended to be a particular target for the iconoclast; its survival in situations such as this is a comparative rarity in this country.

As to major pieces of work, six figures to the Abbot's Gate (now gateway to the Bishop's Palace) – three to the north and three to the south – are important. Those to the south represent the Cathedral's patron saints. To the outer public face are a mitred abbot (**9**), a prior and, up in the gable, a king (**10**). The latter may be Edward II who, as future king, and with his favourite Piers Gaveston, 'were entertained very nobly' by Abbot Godfrey of Crowland, who completed the Gate. Sheltering in their deep niches, these figures have fared much better than most of those on the Cathedral's West Front, and must be of national importance as externally surviving Gothic sculpture of around 1300.

13

The medieval carver in stone and wood might often be allowed a fairly free rein when it came to choice of subject matter. On the outside of churches, particularly at high level, the constraints could be even less than those imposed, say, upon woodcarvers working on misericords inside. Medieval churches can still be found bristling with fantastical creatures – a veritable menagerie of strange composite life forms pouring forth from the medieval ark or, more precisely, from bestiaries. The gargoyle (strictly speaking only such if functioning as a water spout) is one of the most frequent recipients of such fanciful treatment (**12**).

PREVIOUS PAGE

11 Glinton
12 Castor
13 Glinton

THIS PAGE

14 Maxey
15 Maxey
16 Glinton
17 Etton

17

Glinton church sports a fine array of functioning examples (**11**). On the south side three assorted beasts discharge their practical function in the usual way but the last, to the east, goes about it in an altogether different manner (**13**). Medieval humour tended towards the coarse rather than the keen; scatological references are not uncommon. Maxey's gargoyles offer a similar mixture, from the functionally straightforward (**14**) to this headless example (**15**), now probably functionally redundant, but destined to be priapic in perpetuity.

High on Etton church tower a corbel table frieze of notch-head masks, little faces and *fleurs de lys* ends, somewhat improbably, with a *sheela-na-nig* (**17**). (The term seems to have been borrowed from the Irish by Victorians in search of a euphemism.) The precise meaning of such grotesque female figures, whether fertility symbols from a pagan past, warnings against lechery or simply mason-carvers just having fun, remains a subject for endless debate. They tend, usually, to be associated with Romanesque buildings, whereas Etton church seems entirely of the 13th century. Moreover the flattened head and horizontal position (no jokes please!) also suggest that the figure may not be *in situ*, although it seems to be of a piece with the moulding above.

18

19

20

22

23

21

THIS PAGE

18 Bainton: St Mary
19 Minster Precincts: Infirmary
20 Minster Precincts: Infirmary
21 Thorpe Hall: garden wall
22 Thorney Abbey
23 Thorney Abbey
24 Thorney Abbey

24

The task of establishing the likely dates and meaning of bits of carving found on the outside of buildings can be fraught with difficulty. Perhaps the chief complicating factor is the past propensity for relocating salvaged bits and pieces in wholly unconnected contexts as ornament. Then there are issues surrounding restoration work and the revival of historic styles.

The (12th-century?) bust of a lady in Bainton church porch (**18**) is clearly not *in situ*; she has, however, acquired a splendid additional headdress of chicken-netting. Two corbelled stops from what was the Peterborough Abbey Infirmary do remain in their original locations (**19** and **20**). The three faces to one head may be another visual representation of the Trinity. Medieval mouldings visible to the inner face of Thorpe Hall's garden wall

(**21**) furnish evidence for the removal of quantities of material from the Cathedral Precincts in the 1650s and its reuse here.

A series of carvings from a frieze at Thorney Abbey (**22**, **23** and **24**) may appear, at first glance, to include some of the cast of curiosities from the medieval menagerie. But step back a little; the context is that of the adaptations of 1638 around the west doorway (page 25, number **45**) where it seems Gothic Survival meets Gothic Revival. So the curiosities in the frieze are but an unintended parody of the stuff of the bestiaries. Also from Thorney Abbey is a grimacing mask (king-cum-beast?) forming a large label-stop (**25**). This represents a still later attempt at resurrecting the spirit of medieval grotesquery, belonging as it does to Edward Blore's Neo-Norman additions of the 1840s.

Not quite *in situ*, though it probably hasn't moved far, is the corbel of a mason (his mason's mark above) within the semi-ruined former Peterborough Abbey Infirmary (**26**). It is tempting to believe that this is the master mason who, with his Winchester connections, was responsible for erecting the huge 13th-century structure. By contrast, the mitred character (**29**), his visage heavily restored, hasn't strayed at all from the Abbey across the road in Thorney, but seems rather to be a bit of 19th-century ornament – a Romantic reference to the mitred abbots of Thorney. Henry VIII louring over the tradesman's entrance to the Cathedral Precincts is a late 20th-century manifestation of the tyrant's infamously thunderous visage (**27**).

THIS PAGE
25 Thorney Abbey
26 Minster Precincts: Infirmary
27 Minster Precincts: Wheel Yard Gate
28 Alwalton
29 Thorney

30

31

32

33

34

THIS PAGE

30 Stanground:
St John the Baptist
31 Fletton: St Margaret
32 Longthorpe
33 Sutton
34 Castor

Church exteriors and churchyards display many decorative permutations on the theme of the cross. A group of pre-Conquest crosses survive in the area. Those at Stanground and Fletton (**30** and **31**) are perhaps the most nearly complete; both exhibit evidence of the characteristic wheel-head cross at the top, together with a pair of lugs or 'handles' to the shaft. A piece of what is held to be an Anglo-Saxon cross-shaft (**33**) is built into the gable-end wall of a dovecote once forming part of the Sutton Grange complex. Its visible face is decorated with a very loose, irregular interlace quite unlike the tight, regular patterns of the Longthorpe shaft (**32**) or indeed the relocated tympanum (Christ giving a benediction?) of assumed similar date above the south porch of Castor Church (**34**). The Sutton shaft does, however,

carry a tight cable moulding along its edges similar to that visible (just) on the Fletton example. Noteworthy from Barnack's tower are several decorative slabs with quite unusual foliated scrolls branching from a stem, a bird at the top (**35**).

St Vincent's Cross – 15th century – stood for centuries by the wayside on the road between Thorney and Crowland (**36**). In 1990 the cross was moved, apparently for its safety, from a position about 250m SSW. Its tapering octagonal shaft, now headless, stands on a base with corner 'spurs', a shield on each of the four faces between. Three of the shields carry the remnants of heraldic devices now difficult to interpret; the fourth was either blank or is even more eroded. The cross appears to have originated there to mark a boundary between ecclesiastical

estates settled initially in the late 10th century (though no authentic document before the Conquest gives definitive boundaries) but seemingly the focus of intermittent squabbles over land holdings between the abbeys of Peterborough and Crowland from the 13th century through to their dissolution. It also seems to have marked the confluence of three county boundaries – Soke of Peterborough, Lincolnshire and Cambridgeshire.

   Foliated Gothic gable crosses have seldom survived in their exposed positions without extensive restoration, or, more likely, as with the trio atop the Cathedral's West Front, replication. Nevertheless, whether repaired, restored or revived, many continue, as with the trio here (**37**, **38** and **39**) to cut a dash against the sky.

THIS PAGE

35 Barnack:
     St John the Baptist
36 Thorney/Crowland
37 Eye
38 Maxey
39 Peakirk

40

42

43

41

44

45

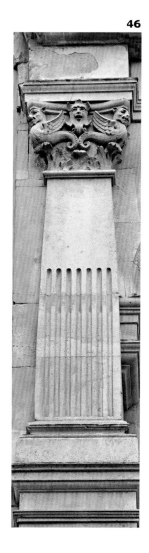

Sundry delights await the observant seeker after carved detail and minor sculpture. From Thorpe Hall's garden comes a spiralling volute (**40**), a strange Ionic column sprouting from acanthus in a niche (**41**) and a scowling lion on an urn (**42**). The carving on a former pub on the corner of Cowgate and Cross Street takes the most extremely fanciful liberties with the Classical Orders (**44**, **45** and **46**). And very enjoyable they are too.

A closer look at a gable seen earlier (**43**) reveals a quite astonishing collection of carved detail, from Ionic colonnettes, a scrolled pediment and medallions to a Vitruvian scroll, shell-hooded niches and all manner of finials. In a wintry landscape at Burghley a finely carved lion couchant guards 'Capability' Brown's Lion Bridge of 1775 (**47**). The sheep in the distance carry on regardless.

PREVIOUS PAGE

40 Thorpe Hall: Garden doorway
41 Thorpe Hall: Garden gate pier
42 Thorpe Hall: Garden
43 Cathedral Square/Bridge Street
44 Cowgate/Cross Street
45 Cowgate/Cross Street

THIS PAGE

46 Cowgate/Cross Street
47 Burghley: Lion Bridge

THIS PAGE

48 Lincoln Road
49 Lincoln Road
50 Lincoln Road
51 Lincoln Road

NEXT PAGE

52 Cathedral Square
53 Cathedral Square
54 Cowgate

51

A late 19th-century house in Lincoln Road, set at a surprising angle to the street frontage, catches the eye for its display of carving in stone, brick and wood. In the gable, housed in a niche beneath carved bargeboards, is a *putto* (a complete wingless cherub) (**48**) holding a painter's palette and brush. A different gable carries a panel of carved brickwork (**49**) – cherubs of another sort this time. Above the doorway a carved panel (**50**), recently dramatically painted, depicts a hunting scene – a young boy trumpeting while running with dogs. Focussing down closer (**51**) one is surprised to find in the background a representation of the Cathedral West Front.

49

PEADA
KING·OF·MERCIA

ATHWALD
BISHOP·OF·WINCHESTER

All of this decorative workmanship becomes clearer with the realisation that, for about twenty-five years until his death in 1913, Clyde House was home to Walter Allan '...the well-known sculptor...quite a genius in his profession...', winner of many medals and awards. It would appear that many of Allan's commissions came from Messrs Hitch and Nicholls, London carvers in stone and wood who worked regularly for J L Pearson, Cathedral architect towards the end of the 19th century. It seems possible therefore that some of Allan's work was intended for the Cathedral; indeed some might be there.

From the former Boots building of 1911 (see page 50, number **35** for more detail on this 'curiosity') come two representatives from its cast of 'local' *dramatis personae* – Peada, first (even if short-lived) Christian King of Mercia (**52**) and St Aethelwold, Bishop of Winchester and putative refounder of the Abbey in the late 10th century (**53**). Whether these figures are carved in wood or, in view of all the surrounding pargetted plasterwork, are modelled in plaster built up on a frame, is difficult to tell. A few hundred yards away in Cowgate another building listed solely for its 'curiosity value' is Nelson House (**54**). A rather fine bust of the great admiral housed in his eponymous niche high on the façade must be the principal 'curiosity', though he is accompanied by quite an arresting assemblage of elaborate console brackets, and some decent cast ironwork.

Ironwork and Ironmongery

Ironwork has long had both a functional and a decorative role in architecture and construction. Essentially there are two basic types: wrought iron (workable by hand, malleable when heated and capable of being formed into ornamental scroll and filigree work) and cast iron (cast in moulds, weak in tension but strong in compression and therefore capable of much structural as well as decorative usage). Much modern work along the lines of 18th-century decorative wrought ironwork is more likely to be formed in mild steel, which is capable to an extent of being worked cold.

Ironmongery too is included here. Metal fixings of one sort or another – hinges, knockers, locks, escutcheons, bolts,

bell-pushes and a whole range of fastenings, these – and small features such as gates often combining cast and wrought work – complete the picture. Ironmongery may well, of course, contain metals other than iron.

With the arrival in Britain of Jean Tijou shortly after the Revocation, in 1685, of the Edict of Nantes the whole concept of wrought ironwork was transformed, adding to an already well developed art something of the panache and bravura of the France of Louis XIV and thereafter raising the craft here to a pre-eminent position in Europe. Alongside celebrated work by Tijou at Chatsworth, Hampton Court and St Paul's Cathedral stands his work at Burghley.

PREVIOUS PAGE

1 Cathedral

THIS PAGE

2 Burghley
3 Burghley
4 Thorpe Hall

5

6

7

Celia Fiennes, the indefatigable traveller, opinionated travel writer and inveterate touristic busybody, offers the following in the account of her travels between 1685 and 1703, which can only refer to Tijou's Golden Gates on Burghley's west front (**2**): '... The door on top of the Stepps is of iron carv'd, the finest I ever saw, all sorts of leaves, flowers, figures, birds, beast, wheat, in the Carving; very large the doors are.'

Much fine ironwork survives at Burghley, both surrounding the great house and at some distance within its park. Precisely who smithed this considerable output is not entirely clear, though it has recently been suggested that Tijou was responsible for the north court gate. At any event much of the ironwork would do credit to any one of a number of nationally famous names.

Amongst details illustrated here are overthrows such as **3** and **5**, gilded finials, both cast and wrought, the latter topped with coronets (**6**) and an elaborate device in wrought scroll-work to deter climbers attempting a traverse of the wall above the ha-ha (**8**).

In the same spirit are details of two more overthrows: one from Thorpe Hall (**4**), the other to the Cathedral porch, much gilded, and, since its gates are not full height within the opening, with the luxury of more elaborate scroll-work beneath the supporting cross-bar carried on piers (**1**). The spirit of 18th-century wrought ironwork, even if mild steel may be involved, is captured in 20th-century work in Lincoln Road (**9**) and, half hidden in the boscage, behind Peterscourt (**10**).

PREVIOUS PAGE

5 Burghley
6 Burghley
7 Burghley

THIS PAGE

8 Burghley
9 Lincoln Road
10 Wheel Yard
11 Peakirk

12

13

14

15

16

THIS PAGE

12 Milton Ferry Bridge
13 Exchange Street
14 Minster Precincts
15 Ufford
16 St Peter's Road
17 Orton Waterville

NEXT PAGE

18 St Peter's Road
19 Peakirk
20 Etton
21 Maxey
22 Eye
23 Barnack

17

Wrought and cast iron appear together in all manner of railings and gates, domestic and otherwise, sometimes in conjunction with wood (**12**), and are held together and operate with some fascinatingly detailed fastenings and catches. On the north side of St John's Church in the city centre a long run of spear-headed railings (**13**) – twisted standards with curved supporting stays punctuating the long perspective – survive to perpetuate the memory of similar runs recently removed from the south and west sides.

Elsewhere (**14**) plain stick balusters to a handrail have each been given a couple of twists to add a bit of minimal wrought decoration and interest. A pretty Regency or early Victorian porch from Peakirk (**19**) appears to be constructed mainly of cast iron, including the Gothick quatrefoiled spandrels and intersecting pattern balcony railing, with rows of miniature quatrefoils to its top and bottom rails.

18

20

22

21

19

23

24

25

PRESENTED TO THE CITIZENS OF PETERBOROUGH
JUNE 22 1931
BY
PERCY MALCOLM STEWART ESQUIRE

26

THIS PAGE

24 East coast main line
Nene Bridge
25 Priestgate: Museum
26 Rivergate

NEXT PAGE

27 Burghley
28 Exchange Street
29 Fletton
30 Welland Road
31 Alwalton
32 Rivergate
33 Orton Waterville
34 Rivergate
35 Newborough

Unquestionably the most spectacular structural use of cast iron in Peterborough is in the three great spans which carry the main east coast rail route across the River Nene (**24**). Each span has three pairs of segmental arched girders, diagonal lattice work in the spandrels, carried, mid-stream, on a total of twenty-four mighty fluted Greek Doric iron columns. The whole ensemble is not only a piece of railway engineering of national significance, but also has a considerable architectural presence. (The severe Greek Revival style may also be seen not far away in the portico at the entrance to the Museum [**25**]. Here of course the order is executed in stone, but is surmounted with a pretty iron railing with rectangles containing diamond fret patterns.

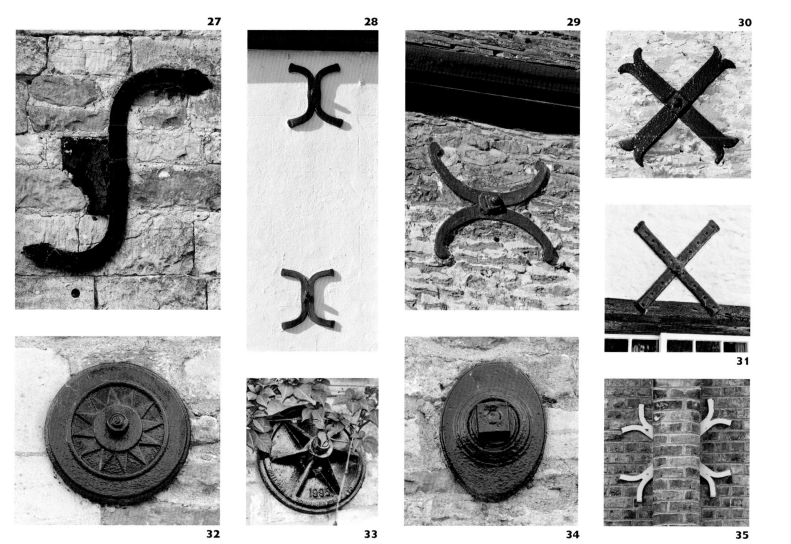

The numbers 31, 32, 33, 34, 35 label the images.

Such patterns were used in ironwork from the beginning of the 18th century, and are still being used here in the Regency.)

The great cast iron bridge, believed to be the last surviving in Britain to carry a major high speed rail route, was constructed in 1850 for the Great Northern Railway, probably to the designs of the engineer Joseph Cubitt. The involvement in major projects of a whole dynasty of Cubitts (father Sir William, son Joseph and nephews Lewis and Thomas), not least in constructing the Great Northern, is further complicated by the fact that even in the mid 19th century the distinction between the roles of architect and engineer remained somewhat blurred; individual Cubitts are variously identified as either or both.

The contractor for the bridge's construction was the celebrated Thomas Brassey, builder of railways the world over.

Another, more prosaic constructional use of cast and wrought iron is for the plates at the ends of ties threaded through a structure to restrain deformed or leaning walling. Image **31** shows that it may not always be possible to thread a tie through at the best place from the point of view of appearance. The completion, in 1995, of a scheme of conservation repair by Bowmans of Stamford appears to be celebrated by **33**. Quite how the tie plate (**35**) came to be hiding behind a buttress is unclear.

36

37

38

Although much fine medieval wrought ironwork survives nationally – chiefly internally around tombs, chantry chapels, etc., but also in the form of decorative door hinges and ornamental door furniture – so far as we can see nothing of significance that is externally visible seems to have survived locally, even in fragmentary form. However, the Gothic Revival had little difficulty in finding exemplars; a sample of their progeny is included here (**36–38**).

THIS PAGE

36 Eye: St Matthew
37 Eye
38 Etton

NEXT PAGE

39 Eye
40 Orton Waterville
41 Orton Longueville
42 Wothorpe
43 Werrington
44 Alwalton
45 Wentworth Street

46 Broadway
47 Thorney
48 Werrington
49 Eye
50 Thorpe Hall
51 Marholm: St Mary

39 40 41 42 43 44 45 46 47 48 49 50 51

52

54

55

53

56

A surprising use for iron is in the churchyard at Marholm, where the burial place of Robert Vergette and his wife is commemorated with a cast iron lid to their tomb chest (**52**). Robert was brother to George Vergette who ran an ironmongery business on the south side of what is now Cathedral Square in the 19th century. At the foot of the casting is the *memento mori* of a winged hourglass: *Tempus* literally *Fugit*. (The Vergette stamp can be found on a repair to the Thorpe Hall gates (page 12, number **1**).

To stumble upon the gates fronting the 13th-century hall house adjoining Longthorpe Tower, and there to encounter their unusual blazons of heraldry (**54**), may induce puzzlement. Until, that is, their Italian baronial nature is explained, a manifestation of Peterborough's thriving Italian community.

Today, railings, gates, handrails, balustrading and so forth may well be fabricated from mild steel bar or even tubing, with any ornamentation as likely to be cast in aluminium as in iron. Stainless steel is also widely exploited, as with the shiny new handrail on the approach to the tower entrance of St John's (**53**). At St Paul's, New England, the iron finial crowning the pyramidal tower roof had become unsafe and has been replaced by a gleaming new stainless steel cross (**55**). A surviving iron cross

atop the apse may be seen in the lower right foreground.

A recent addition to the palette of constructional metals is weathering steel (usually referred to by its brand name Corten steel). Designed to eliminate the need for painting, it forms a stable rust-like protective layer on its surface when weathered. Peterborough's Shanks Millennium Bridge at Northey Bank (**57**), part of the Green Wheel cycleway and linking eastern Peterborough with Whittlesey, is constructed principally of Corten steel. Designed by leading bridge engineers Whitby Bird & Partners, it incorporates some stylish details and was a 2003 RIBA award winner.

PREVIOUS PAGE

52 Marholm
53 St John's Square
54 Longthorpe
55 New England: St Paul's
56 Gladstone Street

THIS PAGE

57 Northey Bank

1

Street Furniture

Street Furniture comes in all sorts of shapes and sizes erected by different authorities with seemingly little thought to the overall effect on the streetscape. Objects range from sign posts to bollards, litter bins to bus shelters, lamp posts to parking meters. For the purposes of this book we are confining ourselves to a few types of street furniture – mainly examples which have proved the most enduring.

A typical piece of street furniture is, of course, the bench such as (**2**), an elegant seat in the newly remodelled Cathedral Square (works completed 2011). The blocks (**3**) are also part of the new Cathedral Square scheme, serving as street dividers as well as basic seats. A more traditional seat is the park bench. This one (**4**) in Central Park, very unusually, is dedicated to

2

3

4

several Kurdish people with Peterborough connections who were killed in Saddam Hussein's massacre of the inhabitants of the town of Halabja during the Iran-Iraq war in 1988. Benches in the countryside such as (**5**) can be nice examples of rustic joinery.

PREVIOUS PAGE

1 Upton

THIS PAGE

2 Cathedral Square
3 Church Street
4 Central Park
5 Alwalton

5

6

7

8

THIS PAGE

6 Thorpe Road
7 Westgate
8 Wothorpe

Pillar boxes have been part of the townscape for well over a hundred years and obligingly express their allegiance to their monarch. The Victorians are here represented by the example in Thorpe Road (**6**). In the city centre **7** appeared in the reign of George VI. In the rural areas we find an alternative to pillar boxes – post boxes set into walls of buildings. **8** is of Victorian vintage, **9** Edwardian, **10** early 20th-century, and **11**, post-1953.

As more of us carry mobile phones, the demand for public telephone boxes has declined and many have been removed and sold as garden ornaments or scrap. But there are survivals, usually listed or in Conservation Areas, some still serving their original purpose, others not. The example at Thornhaugh (**12**) has a new use as a book exchange for the villagers.

The phone box made its debut in 1921 and from the late 1930s was to be found everywhere. At the height of its reign at least 20,000 examples existed on British streets. Two versions of this kiosk, one in 1924 and the final version, the K6, of 1935, were to designs by Sir Giles Gilbert Scott (the grandson of 'Great Scott') who in 1903, when still in his early twenties, had won the competition to design Liverpool's Anglican Cathedral. (A K6 still functions inside the Cathedral at the foot of the tower.) Less well-known is the fact that the K6, a design classic, was inspired by the strange mausoleum designed by Sir John Soane (arguably England's most original Neoclassical architect) for himself and his wife in St Pancras Old Churchyard, London.

THIS PAGE

9 Woodston
10 Thornhaugh
11 Ufford
12 Thornhaugh

13

14

15

THIS PAGE

13 Glinton
14 Sutton
15 Ufford
16 Thornhaugh
17 Peakirk
18 Cathedral Square

NEXT PAGE

19 Castor
20 Alwalton
21 Orton Waterville
22 Lincoln Road
23 London Road
24 Wheel Yard
25 Wansford Bridge
26 Alwalton

16

1837. VICTORIA .1901.
ERECTED BY VOLUNTARY CONTRIBUTIONS

17

18

23 **24** **25** **26**

Public watering points usually only survive as relics. There are a few non-functioning village pumps in our area, usually locally cast, including those at Glinton, Sutton and Ufford (**13**, **14** and **15**). We have not found any surviving water troughs for horses, but an unusual low-level 'fountain' is set into a wall opposite the former Thornhaugh village school (**16**) (a water trough for dogs?). And a drinking trough survives in Peakirk – commemorating Queen Victoria's reign (**17**). The only working street fountains in the Peterborough area are the impressive water features that are the key element of the restored Cathedral Square (**18**).

Milestones and boundary marker stones were, no doubt, once commonplace but now fairly rare. The stone milestones at Castor (**19**) and Alwalton (**20**) are badly weathered. The examples from Lincoln Road (**22**) and London Road (**23**) are cast iron rather than stone but deserve maintenance attention. At first sight (**25**) seems to be a milestone but is, in fact, a marker on the bridge at Wansford to indicate the boundary between the former county of Huntingdonshire and the Soke of Peterborough. A modern less subtle version at Alwalton (**26**), marks the boundary between Peterborough City Council Unitary Authority and Huntingdonshire District Council.

28

THIS PAGE

27 Helpston
28 Bainton
29 Helpston

NEXT PAGE

30 Peakirk
31 New England
32 Bishops Road
Gardens
33 Marholm
34 Bridge Street

At one time almost every village in the land would boast a village cross, churchyard cross or, especially if covered, a buttercross. Our examples include crosses at Helpston and Bainton (**27** and **28**) and the more recent village cross at Peakirk (**30**). The latter is inscribed 'E J 1904', it refers to the Revd Ernest Jones, Rector of St Pega's at Peakirk 1865–1912. He had the cross erected at his own expense, perhaps for no other reason than to leave a memento in the village that he ministered to for so many years.

The grandest category of street furniture must be sculptures and monuments. Peterborough's have a habit of wandering about. Much of its public sculpture once in the City Centre

32   33

or local centres has been relocated to the Sculpture Park in Ferry Meadows. But some monuments remain. The Ball Memorial Fountain at the New England Triangle (**31**) was erected by Canon C R Ball, first vicar of St Paul's, and his sisters in memory of their parents and as a gift of gratitude for the happy years spent at 'the Railwaymen's church'. It was unveiled in 1884. Perhaps better known is the Gates Memorial (**32**) commemorating Henry Pearson Gates (1818–93), the first Mayor of Peterborough in 1874. It was erected in Cathedral Square (then Market Place) at the expense of his widow in 1898. Years later, in 1967, having been considered a traffic encumbrance, it was moved to Bishop's Road Gardens.

One of the Peterborough area's most famous sons is John Clare, the 'peasant poet'. He is commemorated in his home village of Helpston by a bold inscription on his memorial (**29**).

War memorials can be found in several of our villages – Thornhaugh, Barnack and Marholm (**33**) for instance. But the most recent is in the city centre, near the Town Hall (**34**). For some years it had been felt that the war memorial in the Cathedral precincts was rather hidden away and not well sited for memorial parades and such like. A fund-raising campaign was mounted to meet the cost of an elegant new memorial unveiled in 2012. The designer was local architect Peter Slinger.

Coats of Arms and Plaques

The primary purpose of plaques of all descriptions is to impart information, whether by means of words, symbols, numerals or all three. Yet coats of arms, whilst offering the greatest scope for visual display, can confuse with ease.

The arms of the Dean and Chapter display crossed swords with crosslets; those of the See – diocese – of Peterborough crossed keys with crosslets. Quite why the same heraldic content is combined on a cartouche dated 1906 at the Peterborough Corporation Waterworks (**4**) is not immediately obvious. It appears that Henry Gates, on being elected the first mayor of the City of Peterborough in 1874 devised the new

THIS PAGE

1   Bridge Street: Town Hall

2

4

THIS PAGE

2 Bishops Road
Gardens

3 Bishops Road
Gardens

4 South of Etton

5 Thorpe Road:
Sessions House

6–9 Cathedral Square:
Guildhall

5

3

6

7

8

9

shield for Mayor, Alderman and citizens of the City, by simply combining the arms of See and Chapter (**3**). Those of the See, on the left as we view it (from the bearer's viewpoint the right, or 'dexter') taking heraldic precedence over those of the Chapter on the 'sinister', or bearer's left. The heraldry on Gates' memorial (**2** and **3**) thus becomes a triple reference to his having held civic office and legal positions with both Chapter and Bishop.

The arms of the See are historically justified on the former Sessions House (**5**) since the gaol once attached thereto had replaced that of the Lord Paramount from 1839 (Lord Burghley having received rights of jurisdiction surrendered by the Bishops under Elizabeth I).

Gates' mayoral arms served the city until the formal grant of new City Arms in 1960. Yet the crossed keys alone and without crosslets was concurrently in civil use (not unreasonably, given the name of the place). They appear in the cartouche within the 1930's Town Hall's pediment (**1**).

A cluster of small coats of arms around the central window of the Guildhall's east elevation (**6–9**) commemorates major donors, ecclesiastical and patrician, who contributed towards the building's erection (or completion) following the Restoration.

10

This building was erected in 1744 by The Hon. Edward Wortley, Esq. Member of Parliament for Peterborough

11

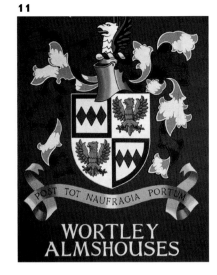

POST TOT NAUFRAGIA PORTUM

WORTLEY ALMSHOUSES

12

THIS PAGE

10 Westgate
11 Westgate
12 Exchange Street/
   Cathedral Square

NEXT PAGE

13 Thorney
14 Cattle Market Road
15 Cathedral Square: Guildhall

One or two of the patrician arms seen on the Guildhall and elsewhere crop up here and there in rather different guises. Witness the splendid pub sign to the Wortley Almshouses (**11**). Close up, the Wortley motto becomes legible; loosely: 'After so many shipwrecks a harbour', or perhaps 'Any port in a storm', as many a *habitué* (including this one) might have it, having survived a shopping expedition in Queensgate. (Sydney Montague, sometime MP and father of Edward whose munificence established the new workhouse here in 1744 [**10**] took the surname of the wealthy heiress he had married.

Was the Wortley wealth the 'harbour' he sought?)

A coat of arms on the later 19th-century Market Chambers (**12**), said originally to have been Peterborough's first department store, incorporates some Fitzwilliam heraldry, indicating development by what is now Milton (Peterborough) Estates Co. Another such coat of arms is round the corner in Long Causeway in the pediment of a building dated 1931.

Royal arms, usually in versions particular to the reigning monarch, are quite numerous too. That at Thorney (**13**) graces buildings erected twenty years or so into Victoria's Reign.

The public entrance to the long-abandoned County Court building in Midgate (built in 1873 for the magistrates of the Liberty or Soke) carries a less personalised version (**14**). But there is no escaping the exuberance with which the Restoration of the monarchy was celebrated at the Guildhall (**15**). Charles II's monogram – CR for *Carolus Rex* – is borne aloft by what appear to be cherubim adopting attitudes familiar from those of the censing angels of the centuries before. It would appear that notions of the divine right of kings still had some little way to run.

16

A.D. 1903
Erected by the Feoffees
out of the fund bequeathed by
MISS FRANCES PEARS
of this City, for the use of the
aged and infirm of the parish of
PETERBOROUGH:

19

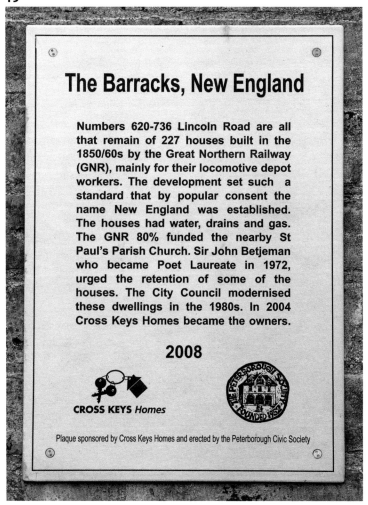

The Barracks, New England

Numbers 620-736 Lincoln Road are all that remain of 227 houses built in the 1850/60s by the Great Northern Railway (GNR), mainly for their locomotive depot workers. The development set such a standard that by popular consent the name New England was established. The houses had water, drains and gas. The GNR 80% funded the nearby St Paul's Parish Church. Sir John Betjeman who became Poet Laureate in 1972, urged the retention of some of the houses. The City Council modernised these dwellings in the 1980s. In 2004 Cross Keys Homes became the owners.

2008

CROSS KEYS *Homes*

Plaque sponsored by Cross Keys Homes and erected by the Peterborough Civic Society

IN THIS COTTAGE JOHN CLARE
THE POET WAS BORN
JULY 13:1793,
THIS TABLET IS ERECTED BY THE
PETERBOROUGH MUSEUM SOCIETY
1921

17   **18**

NATIONAL UNION OF
RAILWAY WOMENS GUILD
PETERBOROUGH
N.1 BRANCH

THIS PAGE

16 Cumbergate
17 Helpston
18 Northfield Road
19 Lincoln Road

NEXT PAGE

20 Bridge Street: Town Hall
21 Bridge Street: Town Hall
22 Thorney
23 Ufford
24 Bainton

Plaques conveying more specific information fall into several categories: those which are decorative as well as commemorative (**16**), those which have a direct utility and are self-explanatory (**17**), those where the conveying of factual information is the prime concern (**19**) and quite a few somewhere in between.

A couple of roundels (**20** and **21** representing Civic Jurisprudence and the Science of Biology) come from a series of ornaments on the Town Hall which also celebrate the range of commercial, agricultural and industrial activity of the mid 20th-century city.

20

21

22

23

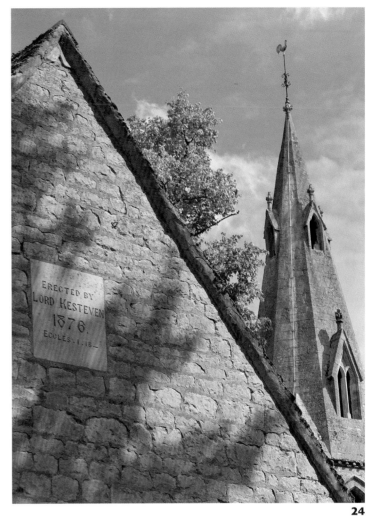

24

Others again have more cryptic content, prompting further inquiry. One such is the little plaque within the gable of a gateway to Thorney Abbey churchyard (**22**). The letters IHC are a variant of the Sacred Monogram or Christogram usually presented as IHS, denoting the first three letters of the Greek name of Jesus. Such contractions or abbreviations were popularised especially by the Jesuits; it comes as a slight surprise therefore to find one on a mid 19th-century adornment to an Anglican churchyard.

Another curiosity is the inscription on a former barn at Ufford (**23**) which might more usually be found on an almshouse.

Clearly Mrs Ruth Edges saw her gift enduring in perpetuity. The Inclosure map of 1799 shows several parcels of land around Ufford as belonging to the Edges Charity. The Charity Commission records Ruth Edges' Charity (objects: an annual payment to the poor of North Witham and biannual payments to six poor gentlewomen) as ceasing to operate in 2008.

Lord Kesteven's biblical reference on Bainton's former schoolroom (**24**) is hardly a call to learning: Ecclesiastes 1.18 reads 'For in much wisdom is much grief: and he that increaseth knowledge increaseth sorrow'.

25

26

THIS PAGE

25 Park Road
26 Cathedral Square:
Guildhall
27 Castor:
St Kyneburgha
28 Lincoln Road

NEXT PAGE

29 Marholm
30 Wansford
31 Barnack
32 Orton Waterville
33 Ufford

27

28

Datestones as such need to be approached with some caution. If one is clearly integral with the building, there is a fair chance that it conveys a reliable construction date. If in the form of an applied plaque, it may not. In some instances this may be blindingly obvious. The date 1653 carried by the plaque to the frontage of Park Road Baptist Church (**25**) is patently not that of the present building (1907) but refers to the foundation of the first local Baptist congregation in the religious turmoil of the mid 17th century. The Guildhall carries the date 1671 on a small shield added in modern times (**26**).

That's fine for a probable completion date for a rebuilding or substantial renovation after the Restoration, but ignores the conjecture that material in the lowest parts of the structure may just possibly survive from the earlier buttercross on the site.

Even a close examination of the famous consecration tablet from Castor Church (**27**) permits a misreading of the date, which at first suggests 1114. Look more closely, however, and it becomes evident that the penultimate numeral is a pair of Xs overlapped, giving 1124. But it is the exceptional state of preservation of this inscription which has caused a few to question its authenticity.

Elegant lettering accompanying a date tends to be a winning combination (**28** and **29**) – the latter example from Marholm providing a particularly beautiful and complex monogram. Late 18th-century Arabic numerals tend also to be particularly elegantly formed – witness **30** (and **31** – the only datestone with a keystone all to itself?) and **32** (pity about the hard raised cement pointing). The datestone with its own personal pediment (**33**) from Newport Farm, Ufford probably furnishes us with a date (1770) for the lunettes with diaper infill (page 137, number **47**).

1

2

3

4

5

6

7

8

Signs and Lettering

A building's name or function is sometimes built in as a feature of its 'face' (**1** and **2**). More often, building names are merely applied signing (**3** and **4**) even when they refer to such major historic events as the two royal burials in the Cathedral – Katharine of Aragon, the first wife of Henry VIII and Mary Stuart, Queen of Scots.

Proud industrial, commercial and municipal concerns of the 19th or early 20th century were more often sufficiently sure of their permanence and solidity to cast their business names into the building fabric. A nice example is the Peterborough Corporation Waterworks frieze at Etton Waterworks (**6**). Not only is it a reminder of the days when local authorities delivered most infrastructure (electricity, gas, water as well

9

10

11

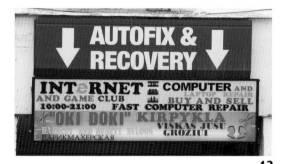

12

13

14

15

16

as roads), but the faintly Art Nouveau lettering style reinforces its 1906 datestone. Non-conformist denominations expressed their reserve with their built-in signs on unassuming chapel buildings (**9**). In contrast, the Jamia Ghousia Mosque boldly incorporates scripture into its fabric (**10**).

Modern signs indicating the use or occupier of a building are usually applied and transient, not least to allow for frequent 'reimaging' or tenancy changes. Yet signing, even when not part of the fabric, can enhance the character of a building (**8** and **15**). The return of symbols indicating the nature of the business harks back to an earlier age when literacy was the exception rather than the rule (**13** and **14**).

PREVIOUS PAGE

1 Aldermans Drive
2 City Road
3 City Road
4 City Road
5 Park Road
6 South of Etton
7 Thorney
8 Exchange Street

THIS PAGE

9 Alwalton
10 English Street
11 Lincoln Road
12 Lincoln Road
13 Long Causeway
14 Fletton
15 Westgate
16 Cowgate

17

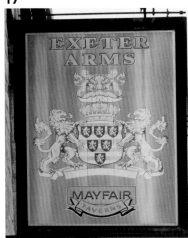

18

19

20

21

THIS PAGE

17 Helpston
18 Eye
19 Helpston
20 Eye
21 Queen's Walk

NEXT PAGE

22 Alwalton
23 Westgate
24 Oundle Road, Woodston
25 West Lake Avenue, Hampton
26 Albert Place
27 Oundle Road, Woodston

Pub signs were originally a means of identifying an inn to travellers and pilgrims. And the sign served to convey its name without the use of written words. Most are long-established and draw their names from the traditional stock of pub names. Some refer deferentially to the lord of the manor (**17**) and others perhaps mark the meeting place of local trades (**18** and **21**). The Beehive (**26**) wittily captures the nature of a more recent bar scene.

22

23

24

25

26

27

28

COUNTY OF
BORO OF
PETER-
BROR
POUGEI

29

ETTON

30

PEAKIRK

31

HAMPTON HARGATE

32

50
1946 1996
DOGSTHORPE
ANNIVERSARY · CELEBRATION

33

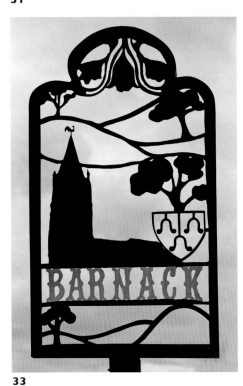

BARNACK

34

APPETITUS RATIONI PAREAT

Marholm

35

HELPSTON

An unusual boundary sign is cast into the concrete bridge carrying the northbound A1 carriageway over the River Nene at Wansford (**28**). An early use of mass concrete in bridge construction and dated 1928, it is one of two signs marking the river as boundary between the then counties of Huntingdonshire and the Soke of Peterborough.

More locally, defining the extent and identity of a neighbourhood is far easier in the rural areas than in urban Peterborough – rural villages have clear geographical limits and a long settlement history. Perhaps that, and the existence of local governance bodies such as Parish Councils, is why there is enthusiasm for the erection of village signs. Women's Institute branches have also been drivers behind the erection of village signs over a long period, especially during anniversary years (Silver Jubilee Year 1977 and the Millennium year for instance). The details of these signs often capture key features of the history or character of the place. The growing focus on urban neighbourhoods may well see these signs adopted in urban Peterborough (**32**).

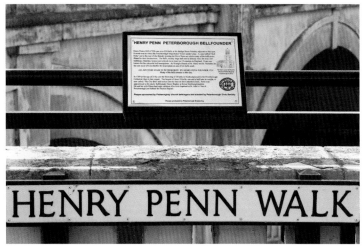

44

45

46

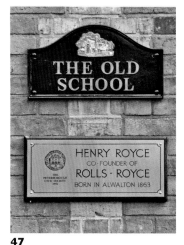

47

48

THIS PAGE

42 Town Bridge
43 Padholme Road
44 Alwalton
45 Bells Place
46 Helpston
47 Alwalton
48 Westgate

Many street names commemorate old field names or those of city dignitaries. Yet when all that remains is the street name-plate, the story of the individual can be lost. The plaque beside the Henry Penn Walk nameplate (**42**) leaves passers-by in no doubt that Henry Penn was a prolific 18th-century bell-founder with a wide reputation. John Clare, the 'peasant poet' (**46**) born in Helpston in 1793 and with a hugely restored reputation since the 1960s, is commemorated in the village sign, a birthplace plaque, the name of the village school, a village monument and John Clare Cottage educational centre. Peterborough Civic Society has arranged for plaques to be placed on over 30 sites in Peterborough and the surrounding villages to commemorate people, events and buildings.

49

50

51

52

53

54

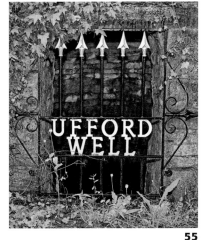

55

56

57

House and farm names provide a window into the diverse range of businesses and services once delivered very locally before the coming of the motor car. The care lavished on the upkeep of the signs behind Peterborough Museum (**51**) enables them to serve as a memorable part of a WWII history lesson.

THIS PAGE

49 Alwalton
50 Orton Waterville
51 Trinity Street
52 Glinton
53 Thornhaugh
54 Eye
55 Ufford
56 Orton Waterville
57 Etton
58 Orton Waterville

58

1

A Miscellany

A final *pot-pourri* of structures, bits of buildings and assorted items which – whether detail or no – contribute to the character or spirit of the place such that we can't resist their inclusion.

Peterborough's somewhat elusive identity, its character perhaps difficult to pin down, arises to a degree from its being a liminal sort of place – a place on the edge, tending to seem on the threshold of somewhere else. Bridges play a prominent role in stressing such liminal attributes, whether as part of the main rail route slicing through the middle of the area roughly along the Fen edge, or crossing the Nene and Welland in places where the rivers define the area's boundary.

Crescent Bridge (**1–5**) is a bow-string lattice span of nearly 50m constructed for the Great Northern Railway in 1913 by

BOTH PAGES

1–5 Crescent Bridge

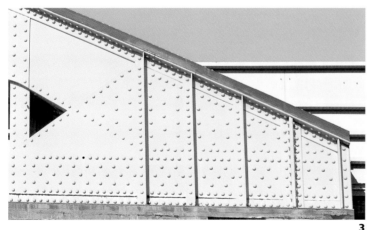

the Cleveland Bridge and Engineering Co. of Darlington. It takes its name not from its shape but from the 1830's crescent of houses once close by the dangerous level crossing, both of which the bridge replaced. For most people approaching Peterborough by road from the west Crescent Bridge may well afford the first glimpse of the Cathedral (**4**).

6

8

7

9

THIS PAGE

6 Castor:
Nene Valley Railway

7 Oundle Road

8 Wansford: A1

9 Ailsworth:
Nene Valley Railway

NEXT PAGE

10 Wansford

11 Deeping Gate

12 Lolham Bridges

A bridge on the first railway route to reach Peterborough (in 1845) suggests the engineer's equivalent of a palaeontologist's Missing Link (**6**). It incorporates both stonework – the preferred material of previous centuries – and brick, heralding the industrial era of bridges incorporating massive hunks of load-bearing brickwork (**7**), iron and, later, steel and concrete (**8**).

Peterborough can lay claim to a half of each of those bridges which span river boundaries (**8, 10** and **11**). Of the twelve spans,

in all, of the splendid ancient bridge at Wansford (**10**), half of the main elliptical (late 18th-century) span, plus ten more (of the late 17th and 16th centuries) on the north bank put their feet (or rather their cutwaters) down on Peterborough soil, only rarely getting them wet. At Lolham Bridges (**12**) a causeway of probably 17th- to 18th-century construction carries the route of Roman King Street (a branch of Ermine Street) across meadows liable to flood adjacent to Maxey Cut.

11

12

13

14

15

16

THIS PAGE

13 Thorpe Hall: garden
14 Thorpe Hall: garden
15 Maxey
16 Orton Waterville

NEXT PAGE

17 Bainton
18 Sutton
19 Burghley
20 Marholm: St Mary
21 Cathedral

Minor structures help to impart character and identity to a place. A couple of details from Thorpe Hall's garden – a pond rim (**13**) and the moulded stone edging to a formal flower bed (**14**) – can scarcely be described as structures at all, but have clearly received care and attention in their design. Small ancillary buildings – a bothy in the Ortons (**16**) or an 18th-century field barn at Maxey, which may have originated as a dovecot (**15**) – give scale to their superiors. Other structures – a sheepwash at Bainton (**17**) and a pound at Sutton (**18**) – tell of former arrangements for animal husbandry.

19

20

21

The haha (**19** and **20**) was a device for maintaining the illusion of cattle grazing in the immediate landscaped parkland without the inconvenience of having to remove their deposits from a well-tended lawn or churchyard.

The flying buttress is designed to transmit a lateral thrust down to a safe place. In medieval architecture it was exploited to a much greater degree by the French in their striving for an aesthetic characterised by dizzying heights. This particular one (**21**), a two-tier affair, was added to the north side of the Cathedral Presbytery only in the first half of the 20th century. The objective was to bolster a pronounced lean which 'Great Scott' (probably, before he was succeeded as Cathedral architect by Pearson) had attempted to arrest by inserting a series of tie-rods about half a century before. It is the Cathedral's only flying buttress. Indeed it is probably the only one in Peterborough, though not far away, at Fotheringhay, the remaining substantial fragment of its former collegiate church positively bristles with them.

22

23

24

25

26

An assortment of structures left stranded by change present themselves. Some have been found a new use. Others, such as the WWII pillboxes beside the Newborough–Thorney Road (**22**) wait patiently for something to come along. And some proudly advance into the future celebrating the ornament of an earlier age.

Long redundant sluice operating gear, a locally cast celebration of Victoria's long reign, has now taken on the mantle of industrial archaeology (**23** and **25**). Recent military hardware (**26**), now just as redundant, has something of the qualities of a sculptural installation about it. A large and grumpy direction sign (**24**) seems to appreciate the imminent complete usurpation of its function by the 'satnav'.

Several brick tower mills in the area have been adapted to residential use. That at Barnack (**27**) has managed to hang on to the blades of its sweeps or sails. At Werrington (**28**) these have gone although the once-rotating cap and fantail survive in replica. On the other hand any hope of an alternative use for the gaunt shell of a windmill tower beside the water meadows of the Nene between Alwalton and Castor (**29**) seems long past.

27

28

29

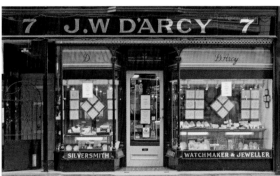

30

31

32

Peterborough is not well endowed with finely detailed shopfronts in the Georgian and Victorian traditions. The D'Arcy shop is a splendid exception (**30**). The rapidity and uncertain direction of change currently overtaking retail shopping may be restrained by the investment being made in the City Centre. More peripheral, mid 20th-century examples are well worth recording (**31**). The pretty little example from Barnack (**32**) with its tiled pastoral scenes to the stall-riser has found a new use.

PREVIOUS PAGE
22 By B1443
23 Maxey
24 Ailsworth
25 Maxey
26 Wittering

THIS PAGE
27 Barnack
28 Werrington
29 Nene watermeadows
30 Westgate
31 Bourges Boulevard
32 Barnack

34

36

37

THIS PAGE

33 Cathedral Square
34 Thorney
35 Minster Precincts
36 Thorney
37 Thorney

NEXT PAGE

38 Taverners Road
39 City Centre 'desire line'
40 Ubiquitous
41 Norfolk Street
42 Bridge Street

Floorscapes of all kinds contribute patterns and textures to the 'feel' of a place. Cathedral Square and its environs have been greatly improved by the scale and patterning of its floorscape (**33**). Yet its quality demands a sustained and intensive cleansing regime.

Less demanding, less heavily used, and much older fragments of nicely textured floorscapes – pitched stones (**34**) or mixtures of pitched stones, cobble and stone setts (**35**) – survive here and there. They can be difficult to date accurately having often been subjected to repeated patch repair. It is tempting to assume that **34** – a pitched stone pathway with central gutter – is a remnant from the monastic buildings on the south side of the Abbey

38

40

41

39

42

church at Thorney, the probable location of its cloister. However it seems more likely that it is of a considerably later, post-Dissolution, date possibly associated with the more prosaic establishment of a market area and shambles.

Almost opposite, the pavement at the entrance to Thorney Abbey (house) is a textured floorscape (**36** and **37**) comprising stone setts and tile nicely offsetting the fine rusticated gate piers. (The detailed touches of the piers hint at the Artisan Mannerism of Thorpe Hall. No surprise since its 'architect', Peter Mills, was almost certainly also involved in the design of Thorney Abbey (house) with John Lovin – builder of the Guildhall – as builder.)

Fancy Victorian mosaic designs and patterns to paths and forecourts, and their later replacements (**38**), finding themselves under pressure from the need to maximise off-street car parking space, are now something of a rarity.

Within modern floorscapes sit an assortment of manhole and duct covers, direction indicators (**39**) and the like. Most in the area seem to be of standard pattern (**40**) though Bridge Street possesses an interesting patented cover (**42**). The Clarksteel cover (**41**) is a Yaxley product. And, sadly, we have not managed to discover a single example of a manhole cover cast by the legendary Thomas Crapper and Co. at the Marlborough Works, Chelsea. (In this respect Oakham has one up on Peterborough!)

The area has its fair share of curiosities. The sentry box (**43**) is not a feature one stumbles over every day outside London. The stone bench (**44**) with its random collection of archaeological bits and pieces including, it seems, some diminutive stone coffins, could only be in Barnack. What looks at first a bit like a wishing well in the forecourt of a pretty group of Helpston almshouses (endowed 1907 by James Bradford JP of Brighton, but born in the village) turns out on closer inspection to house a pump (**45**).

Several adjacent houses in Burghley Road sport bits of architectural salvage (including the sundial on page 144, number **18**). Image **46** shows a niche beneath a 'nodding' (projecting)

ogee and a run of carved frieze; what might be described as examples of the Decorated style of the reign of Edward II. But this is Gothic Revival not medieval stuff. Pondering its origin leads one to suspect that the niche and carving were salvaged from the sweeping away in the 1880s of Edward Blore's short-lived choir screen, apse panelling and other fittings in the Cathedral, preparatory to Pearson's reconstruction of the crossing tower.

Equally short-lived, indeed abandoned before completion, was Pearson's own intended choir screen located further west at the end of his present choir stalls. The stone piers to the intended screen's central gateway remained in their incomplete state in

48

49

50

the Cathedral until 1935 when Pearson's intentions for an enclosed choir (the norm in England) were finally abandoned and the stone piers ended up, somewhat ignominiously, adorning the front gate of a house in Wansford (**47**). (To obtain some idea of Pearson's intentions one needs to visit Bristol Cathedral where his designs for such a screen were successfully implemented to the full.)

Personalising buildings with what are probably best described as bits of Folk Art is legion (**48** – is it Bill or is it Ben? and **50**). A relatively modest dwelling at Alwalton is graced by a gateway with aspirations towards being a thatched churchyard lych-gate (**49**).

PREVIOUS PAGE

43 Burghley
44 Barnack
45 Helpston
46 Burghley Road

THIS PAGE

47 Wansford
48 Etton
49 Alwalton
50 Eye

53

More doors and windows. A substantial castellated stone gateway (**52**) stands towards the southern end of a long wall to St Peter's Road, most of which encloses the garden to the Bishop's Palace. This grand entrance gives access not to the Palace garden but rather to a small building latterly in office use but now offering *bijou* artistic performance and display space. This is the Chauffeur's Cottage; presumably the Mayor's chauffeur not the Bishop's as the Palace complex had its own chauffeur's accommodation added in 1897, to the designs of Sir Edwin Lutyens no less!

A very different sort of doorway, a sumptuous work of art of considerable sophistication in its own right, provides the formal entrance to a mosque (**51**).

Windows containing coloured glass visible from the outside, courtesy of borrowed light, have been glimpsed earlier. From Thorney Abbey comes this kaleidoscopic assemblage of fragments of continental glass (**53**) – probably of Swiss or German origin – some showing characteristic use of yellow or silver stain and vitreous enamel pigments. Formed as a panel and set into clear glazing, it is one of several such in Thorney's nave windows.

From a window to the late 13th-century chancel of Ufford Church (grade 1, but distressingly now redundant) comes this glimpse (**55**) of the strong design and rich palette of colours of early 20th-century glass in an Arts and Crafts idiom. It is said to have been based on cartoons provided by a Miss Erskine

of Stamford, who had suffragette connections. Speculative builders of many inter-war houses commonly added a touch of Arts and Crafts-derived decoration with bits of coloured glass around the front door or windows. Often the colours are strong enough to be enjoyed without much need for internal light (**56**).

An assortment of windows from the 13th to the early 19th century well express the sundry adaptations to alternative usage to which the remains of the former monastic Infirmary have been subjected (**54**). What dominates is the large canted two-storeyed bay with its huge eight-over-eight paned sashes all round. (This house, now in office use, featured prominently in the BBC's 1980s production of Trollope's *Barchester Chronicles*).

PREVIOUS PAGE

51 Gladstone Street
52 St Peter's Road
53 Thorney Abbey

THIS PAGE

54 Minster Precincts
55 Ufford: St Andrew
56 Park Road

57

58

59

60

61

62

THIS PAGE

57 Helpston
58 Barnack
59 Barnack
60 Minster Precincts
61 Northborough
62 Minster Precincts

NEXT PAGE

63 Marholm
64 Barnack
65 Marholm

Funerary monuments in local churchyards and cemeteries deserve their own study. Here are a few headstones and tomb-chests, most in the local palette of materials.

Huge numbers of 18th-century limestone headstones survive, though in many instances their inscriptions are now barely legible. Decorative motifs may include draped funerary urns (right-hand gravestone **57**) or, more typically, po-faced *putti* or cherubs reclining on Baroque ornamentation (**58**) or, a bit later in the century, looking out from the *rocaille* scrollwork characteristic of the Rococo style (**59–62**).

64

At Marholm a squad of nicely patinated limestone tomb-chests of standardised form, pilastered at the corners and lightly wreathed in ivy, line up for inspection (**63**).

Far from being standardised or characteristic is the monument in Barnack churchyard to George Ayscough Booth, Gentleman Cadet at Sandhurst, died aged 21, which adopts the surprising conceit of a fallen palm tree (**64**). The use of the motif in this situation is highly unusual, though the palm features a good deal in decoration all the way from the architecture of ancient Egypt to Neoclassicism and is sometimes incorporated into the capitals of varieties of the Corinithian order. In symbolic terms the palm may represent peace or victory over death.

Boldness of a different sort appears amidst the limestone tomb-chests and headstones of Marholm churchyard. The Vergette family, not content with the originality of a cast iron lid to the tomb-chest of Robert and his wife in 1863 (page 170, number **52**), revisit Marholm in the early 20th century, weighing in this time with some thumping great headstones in polished granites (**65**). That to Edward, fifth son of Robert, is polished red (from the feldspar crystals therein) and therefore possibly from Aberdeenshire.

67

2012 witnessed the successful dismantling and safe storage of the great Portland stone 'mural' from the demolished Bridge House (**66**) pending the finding of an appropriate location for its re-erection. Arthur J Ayres' 1955/6 mural in bas-relief, (incised bas-relief might be more accurate) carries a diverse iconographical scheme celebrating the development of human knowledge and scientific progress. A detail (**67**) depicts Sir Isaac Newton with the 14th-century mathematician and theologian Thomas Bradwardine, of Merton College, Oxford (then a hotbed of academic mathematicians and astronomers) and, very briefly, Archbishop of Canterbury. He is accompanied by a '34 magic square' (all lines of numbers totalling 34); though quite why

Bradwardine is depicted studying or drawing the parvise from the Cathedral's West Front is unclear, as he had died from the Black Death in 1349 a little before its likely construction.

Most public sculpture in Peterborough is post-1970 and as such more likely to be broadly figurative or abstract, rarely closely detailed. From the great collection at Thorpe Meadows, Lee Grandjean's eighteen-foot high figure – The Peterborough Arch – erected in 1988, is a fine example and continues to loom over the Longthorpe Parkway (**68**).

A St George and the Dragon at Peterborough Business Park is a very different matter. Superbly detailed and of more than local significance, it was sculpted by Sir George Frampton RA

PREVIOUS PAGE

66 Formerly Town Bridge
67 Formerly Town Bridge
68 Longthorpe Parkway

THIS PAGE

69–72
Peterborough Business Park

in 1919 as a memorial to the fallen of the Pearl Assurance Company In WW1. This fine piece (**72**) (note the pose – shades of Donatello?) was brought to Peterborough in controversial circumstances in 1991 when Pearl moved its headquarters here from London's High Holborn. A couple of details from the pedestal panels, depicting air and sea battles, are also shown (**69** and **70**).

By the early years of the 20th century Frampton had become a sculptor of considerable repute, with a number of monuments to his name in St Paul's Cathedral. He was also responsible (here another tenuous Peterborough connection) for the figure sculpture on the huge monument to Nurse Edith Cavell close to St Martin-in-the-fields.

73

74

77

75

76

THIS PAGE

73 Viersen Platz
74 Mayors Walk
75 East Station Road
76 Near Pilsgate
77 Nene Valley Railway

NEXT PAGE

78 Orton Mere

For a city whose 19th-century growth and development from relative obscurity was propelled largely by the coming of the railways, significant tangible remains from their earlier days are becoming alarmingly thin on the ground, and the future of some of what does remain seems uncertain.

Happily, about half of 'The Barracks' at New England survive to make a significant contribution to the city's housing stock. Built in the 1850s and 60s to house mainly GNR locomotive depot workers, it was an enlightened scheme setting new standards in the provision of working-class housing, hence the adoption of the name for the immediate area: New England. GNR warehouse sheds survive in the city centre, modern

alternative uses necessitating some modifications to their fenestration (**73**). Just north of the centre the GNR Carpenters Shop of *c.*1850 survives, and in some degree of beneficial use. Constructed of gault brick, away from the street frontage the building retains its cast iron glazing bar casements beneath wide red brick segmental arches (**74**)

Close to the south bank of the Nene, substantial remnants of the Peterborough East Station complex, in the form of a Victorian railway engine shed with adjoining goods shed, hang on patiently waiting for a new use (**75**). Built initially for the Eastern Counties Railway in 1858 as a six-track engine shed it is a rare and largely original building (the sort

of structure which cries out to be adapted to provide economical, multipurpose, performance space).

With so much of the familiar paraphernalia associated with that original rail infrastructure – signalling apparatus and the like (**76**) – now disappearing fast, it will not be long before all of what remains in functioning order is likely to be confined to heritage rail routes (**77**). How fortunate we are then to have one of the very best of these, Nene Valley Railway, on our doorstep. Our final image (**78**) celebrates this with a shot of the working signal box at Orton Mere which started life as a crossing-keeper's cabin.

Afterword

Much in this book has reminded us of the rapidity and scale of change during the last century or so; change which shows little sign of diminishing, even through economic down-turns.

To reflect on our heritage of buildings: Fletton Towers in Woodston was once the home of LP Hartley, author of *The Go-Between* (1953). The prologue opines:

> *The past is a foreign country; they do things differently there*

Well yes they do, or rather they did, but the trick in the future will be to recognise and honour that fact while managing the increased rapidity of change in an intelligent and imaginative way, so as to secure new beneficial uses for surviving 'heritage assets' which respect their integrity, character and intrinsic merits.

The potential pitfalls awaiting us as we attempt to pull off such a trick have been the subject of much heated debate since William Morris's polemical diatribes (some aimed in the direction of Peterborough) in the late 19th century. They are perhaps encapsulated in another aphorism anticipating Hartley's, this time from the American writer Christopher Morley:

> *Life is a foreign language; all men mispronounce it.*

Morris held that '...these old buildings do not belong to us only... they will belong to our descendants unless we play them false. We are only trustees for those who come after us' (speech to the Society for the Protection of Ancient Buildings, 1889). So, as William Morris urges, we must '... stave off decay by daily care' (from *The Manifesto of SPAB*).

As to new buildings: in the villages surely we all look for careful development respecting – and usually reflecting – the long-established scale, forms, materials and details of each. And, in the heart of Peterborough, if new development is to be celebrated as heritage in the future we will need more outstanding examples of contemporary design and construction, of an integrity and validity of form and function for their own time but which also respect their context. More examples such as, say, the Crown Court building in Rivergate, Monkstone House in City Road, Bayard Place, and Pearl's former HQ at Peterborough Business Park.

Peterborough and its villages deserve no less.